The WORLD at WAR

50 YEARS LATER

Turner Publishing Company

Co-published by Turner Publishing Company
and Mark A. Thompson, Associate Publisher

Copyright © 1997
Turner Publishing Company

The articles and photographs first appeared in
The Daily Star, Oneonta, N.Y.

Author: Sandra Fentiman
Photographer: Julie Lewis
Graphic Designer: Elizabeth A. Dennis

Library of Congress Catalog
Card No. 97-60015

ISBN: 978-1-68162-206-4

Limited Edition

*Cover Photo: At home on Clinton Street in Oneonta,
Samuel Bertuzzi wears his Navy dress blue uniform from
World War II. He holds a photo of himself taken after being
wounded in the South Pacific. (Photo by Julie Lewis)*

Contents

Introduction

This book began when the Associated Press sent out on its wire services an announcement that the 50th anniversary of the Allied invasion of Italy was approaching. The Daily Star's wire editor, Charles Sauer, picked up on it and persuaded me to find veterans for a story. After the success of that first article, he researched battle dates and prepared a possible monthly schedule.

Thanks to the willingness of both veterans and civilians to speak, sharing their private experiences, one story became a series. The two-year series is now a book.

This volume is meant to educate, so that the facts are not forgotten. My heartfelt thanks go to every person who spent time and effort contributing to this book in some way. Special thanks go to Julie Lewis for her photographic skills, and to those who loaned personal photos.

Lastly, this book is meant as a tribute to those who sacrificed and suffered, and to honor the millions who died.

Sandra Fentiman
January 1997

The World At War 50 Years Later

Memories Of Italy 1943

The uniform patch of the American 5th Army.

When Kurt Langel left the Mediterranean and landed in Italy 50 years ago, he never thought he would be spending much of the rest of World War II far to the north near the Baltic Sea.

There were days when the going seemed uphill all the way; not only the terrain, but morale as well.

It was Italy, 1943.

With the Anglo-American invasion that began 50 years ago this month, the Allies engaged in battles with the Germans for the first time on the European continent.

Langel of Richfield Springs was captured after the Allies invaded Anzio. "We'd gone 25 or 30 miles behind the lines, and we were surrounded by the German Hermann Goring Division," he said. "I don't know if the whole division was there, but it seemed like it. It lasted all one night and all through the next day, and they finally got us.

"I was wounded and they put me in the hospital, and when I recuperated I guess everybody else was gone. I really don't know what happened to a lot of the people," he said.

"I was leaning on a wall and this artillery shell landed close to me. I didn't get any shrapnel wounds, but I got two cuts on my head and one cut on my arm. So it wasn't a life-threatening thing, but it was enough to knock me unconscious and when they got there I couldn't do a darn thing about it. So they hauled me off to a hospital and I was there for two days. Then they put me on a train and took me out of Italy and into Germany."

The British and American strategists disagreed at the time about whether to continue major offensive operations in the Mediterranean, which the British wanted, or shift resources to the United Kingdom and make an attack across the English Channel, which Americans favored.

According to Dr. Richard Schadt, professor of history at the State University College at Oneonta, the fighting between Allied and German forces in Tunisia, Northern Africa, delayed the invasion from Britain.

"It was a very hard fight in Tunisia," Schadt said. "It wasn't over until May of 1943." But since

Some played a support role

In a supporting role during World War II, removed from direct action, were men such as Charles Traphagen. Serving as a meteorologist as part of the 12th Weather Squadron for the Air Force, he arrived in Italy on June 6, 1944, as Normandy was invaded by Allied forces.

"We landed in Naples and they sent us over to Bari, over on the Adriatic coast," the 80-year-old Delhi man recalled. "We took over an Italian farm and laid down steel mats. We furnished weather information for two B-24 outfits."

The steel mesh mats were used to form a runway about a mile long, where bomber groups that later targeted German oil refineries were trained. The farm was turned into a weather station.

"We brought in weather by codes," Traphagen said. "A certain number would mean barometric pressure, another one would mean winds aloft." Weather reports were received and sent out on teletype machines.

"Before the mission, we'd have to brief the flyers on the weather conditions for obvious reasons, so they could see the targets," he said. 'The weathermen could not fly, the reason being not that they were so concerned with our lives, but they needed our services. It was pretty safe, country club conditions, so to speak."

Traphagen stayed there until May of 1945, then was sent to the King of Italy's castle near Naples, where he worked in communications.

Donald Close of Colliersville was another behind-the-scenes man in Italy in 1944. After enlisting in the Army at age 18, he served as an Army Air Force Supply Technician in the 331st Air Service Squadron of the 15th Air Force. Now 70, Close suffers from Parkinsons Disease, according to his wife, June, who married him in 1948.

On the way to Italy, Close's ship stopped briefly in Benghazi, Libya.

"When they were getting their camps set up there, he said, the natives would steal everything that wasn't nailed down," June Close said. "He kept inventory of parts of planes, and did clerk work."

Close spent time at Bari, Anzio and Rome, and had contact with native Italians, sometimes being invited to people's homes for dinner, along with his Army compatriots.

"They camped together for three years," June Close said. "They really became closer to each other than to their own families."

On Sept. 10 Close got to see soldiers he hadn't seen in 50 years. A reunion of his squadron was held in Peoria, Ill., and he attended with June and their son, Jim.

"The colonel had this great big book and he was showing Don," June Close said. "There was this plane in a picture, when radar was new and a super secret thing."

About 50 squadron members were there, and plan another meeting next year in Mississippi. "Don has always talked about the people," she continued. "He said on the way back it was the best trip he ever took."

General George Marshall thought invading Western Europe through France was the way to defeat the Nazis, a huge number of troops weren't committed to the Italian campaign.

"What we wanted was a long summer campaign season, not a winter campaign in Europe," Schadt said. So Operation Overlord, invasion of Western Europe, was postponed until 1944. The invasion of Sicily was held the summer of '43 and took 38 days. It provided the stepping stone to Italy.

"The Italian forces on Sicily collapsed very quickly," Schadt said. "The Italian government removed Mussolini."

Italy surrendered before the actual invasion. But because Hitler had been suspicious that Italy might make peace with the Allies, he had sent troops to occupy the mainland on the pretext of helping the Italians.

"The landing at Anzio was horrible in casualties," Schadt said. "The Germans were able to fight a very slow withdrawal all the way up the peninsula," aided by the rough terrain in the Apennine Mountain range.

Langel served as an Army Ranger, one of a small unit of specially trained soldiers who carried on surprise raids behind enemy lines in Italy.

"We burned gasoline supplies and bridges, stuff like that," said Langel, now 68. "And any other dirty jobs that came along. We did a lot of recon(naissance) work."

Generally the Rangers operated with five or six men in a team, often sneaking through enemy lines, said Langel, who served under General Mark Clark in Africa, Sicily and Italy.

"The Rangers were never meant to be like the infantry, where you would attack a town and hold it," he said. "We came and went, that was about it."

Langel spent a couple of months in a prison camp, then was shipped to Pomerania in the Polish Corridor, near the Baltic Sea. Once there, he and other Americans, Frenchmen and Russians were sent to work farms.

"That's all we did, just farm labor," he said. "It wasn't slave labor, but they expected a full day's work." The irony was that Langel was born in Berlin, Germany, and had lived there until he was seven. As a prisoner of war he was 21 years old and could still understand the language to some degree.

"I never let on that I could understand or speak German, because I heard a lot more that way," he said.

After 14 months as a prisoner, in April 1945 as the war in Europe was nearing its end, the Germans marched their prisoners 2,100 miles at the urging of the International Red Cross, to remove them from a line of Russian attack.

"It was a cold April — there was still snow on the ground," Langel remembered. "We had Army guards with us. They'd confiscate a barn and we'd all sleep in the barn, and in the morning we all got fed and we took off for the day, and the next day we did the same thing again. When I got all done with that I weighed 115 pounds. My average weight at the time was 165."

Kurt Langel (right) who served as an Army Ranger in Italy, and Wilmer Crumb of Morris talk in Crumb's house in Morris about their war-time experiences. Crumb served in the 85th Infantry Division of the 5th Army in Sicily and Italy. (Photo by Julie Lewis)

Toward the end of that journey Langel was able to escape, which he said wasn't hard to do.

"I stayed hidden for three days and at the end of three days our lines came to where I was and I identified myself and that's how I got out," he said. "I looked out of this barn window and I saw American trucks with the white star. I just waved; I still had parts of my uniform on and I still had my dog tags and there was no question. They put me on a truck and gave me something to eat."

From there he went to Belgium, France and home.

"I feel that I was lucky to have been a prisoner of war there, instead of in the Pacific," Langel said. "Those guys really had it bad."

But in spite of seeing some cruelty on the part of SS officers, Langel didn't harbor bad feelings for the German public.

"The people themselves, I don't believe there's a heck of a lot of difference between Germans, the French, or anybody else, mostly," he said.

In spite of all the hardship and hand-to-hand fighting, Schadt said that the Italian campaign didn't have as large an impact as later events in the war.

"That fight went on all during '44 and through the spring of '45," Schadt said. "It was always a side show, compared to the landing in Normandy and where the fighting in Normandy went on. But if you were caught up in the fighting, it was very tough fighting."

Fighting A War From The Skies

J. Paul George

In the skies over Nazi Germany, J. Paul George rushed to save his friend's life. The bombardier, sitting in the nose of a B-17 bomber, had been knocked out by a bullet that grazed him across the head.

"So I got him over to the escape hatch, which was jammed and I had to kick it out, and I dropped him out and pulled the parachute as he went," George said. "We were at about 30,000 feet and we had to abandon ship, so I pulled his rip cord and sent him out. The next time I saw him was in Atlantic City on the boardwalk. The first thing he did was run up to me and say 'What happened?'"

Only five of the 10-member crew escaped from the plane. It was June 1943.

Many veterans of the air war against Germany have similar stories, including Robert Lawson Sr.

After the United States entered the war, George and Lawson, who grew up in Oneonta, N.Y., and knew each other at Oneonta High School, found themselves members of bombing crews in the European theater of World War II.

Lawson, now 74, was pilot of a B-17 bomber that flew missions over Germany in 1944 and '45. On his 26th mission, in April 1945, he was wounded and sent home on a hospital plane.

"I got a piece of flak that came right through my foot and my navigator took care of me," Lawson recalled. "He bandaged it up and gave me morphine. The co-pilot had to bring the plane in and land it — that was his first time he ever landed it alone. He did a nice job.

"They had me down in the hatchway and I could look right out of the Plexiglas nose. I had my microphone on and I said, 'Knox, put it in easy.' And honestly, I shut my eyes and the next thing I know it was just as smooth and terrific as anything."

It was 50 years ago this month that the Allies waged an air offensive over Nazi Germany.

Of all the war's fronts, the strategic bombing of Germany and German-occupied Europe was the longest and most destructive offensive ever carried out from the air. In its entirety, the efforts lasted from the spring of 1942 through the summer of 1944.

The air attack was seen as a necessary preparation for the invasion of Europe by land.

It inflicted terrible destruction on Germany, causing more casualties on civilians than in any other country.

Great Britain's Royal Air Force bombed at night, and the U.S. Army Air Force bombed in daylight, mainly at military targets.

When they went out on a bombing mission, Lawson said this is how it was done:

The navigator gave the pilot all the flying directions until they approached the IP, or initial point, coming up on the target. The aircraft then was switched to an automatic pilot and the bombardier took over the controls. He aimed the plane at the target, since he could see it but the pilot could not.

"When he released the bombs the plane came back to us. It was all done through an automatic pilot," he said. "It's much different today. But it worked."

Flying in large groups over Europe, the B-17s were targets of German anti-aircraft artillery and fighter pilots.

J. Paul George was on his 12th bombing mission as a B-17 navigator when his plane was shot down over Germany.

"We were on a mission to Hamburg, I believe it was, and flak got us pretty bad on the control services on the tail and we couldn't fly too well," he said. "So we tried to skate around and turn, to go back. And five 190s (German aircraft) lined up behind us and they finished up the job.

"They set the thing on fire, and we had a full bomb load yet, plus half a tank of gas, at least. It was burning pretty good."

After parachuting the injured bombardier out of the plane, George bailed out of the burning B-17 and landed in German territory.

He was met face-to-face by enemy troops, captured and taken to an interrogation center for three weeks.

George, now 74, soberly described the events that followed.

Robert Lawson Sr. and J. Paul George sit among World War II photographs and a uniform of George's in George's home in Oneonta. (Photo by Julie Lewis) 11

Robert Lawson's B-17 in the air during World War II on a mission with the 35 other planes in its group.

The ten members of Robert Lawson Sr.'s B-17 bomber crew in Dyersburgh, Tennessee, in 1944 before being stationed in England. Pilot Lawson is in front, far left.

"It was a small cell, solitary; pretty much bread and water. You get to the point where you're about ready to jump on somebody coming into the cell, to bring something to you — stir crazy, I guess you'd call it."

From the interrogation center, a train carried him to Stalag 3, a prison camp that had four compounds with about 2,000 prisoners of war in each. He stayed there until mid-January.

"The Russians were getting rather close to the camp, and they didn't like that so they moved us out on foot," he said. "What you could carry was what you had. Of course, you didn't have much anyway. We walked for the better part of a week."

The Germans crammed the POWs into boxcars carried on a train for two days without food or water, arriving at Moosburg in Bavaria.

"There were some 40,000-odd POWs there of every shape and description you can think of," George said. "There were Indian Sikhs there, French, anybody you can name who was in the war was involved in that particular POW camp.

"You were under strict supervision, with guards all around the camp. In the original camp they had dogs loose at night, so you didn't want to stick your neck out very much — Doberman pinschers."

Despite having to eat on their own with tiny cook stoves made from tin cans, the men tried to restore a semblance of normalcy in their lives by using a few musical instruments supplied by the Red Cross.

"In some of the camps, they let the enlisted guys work. They didn't let the officers work, anywhere that I know of," George explained. "As a navigator, I was a commissioned officer. They had bands there and played various sports. There was some hockey and basketball; this was courtesy of the Red Cross. If you were lucky, you had a shower once a week. The rest of the time it was Artesian wells that you took your bath in; they were cold, real cold."

While George was imprisoned in Moosburg, the war in the skies continued for Lawson.

Lawson's most frightening moment as pilot came in Belgium when he had to crash-land the plane.

"We had been shot up some, but it wasn't on account of that," he said. "We ran low of fuel and I was trying to get into a base in France. Finally we were reading empty on all four of our tanks and we had to do something. I told the fellas to bail out if they wanted to, but they elected to ride it out. I brought it down in a field on the road to Mons in Belgium.

"You've got to come in with your wheels up. You pick the field and you get committed — you don't changed your mind," he said. "There was a railroad track I had to go over and it's got these poles on it and there's a farmer out there with a horse, and he's plowing. And I didn't have a horn. He saw us coming and pulled over. And there was a big embankment right ahead of us. We stopped about 50 feet from it."

A member of the 91st Bomb Group, Lawson joined the Army infantry in 1940 before getting a commission in 1942. In '43 he trained to be a pilot in the Army Air Corps. It was all Army personnel then; the Air Force was created in 1946, he said.

"We went right to England and flew out of Bassingbourne, just north of London, an hour's ride, roughly," he said.

Lawson remembers being briefed each morning before being sent out on a bombing mission.

"You used to hear these footsteps coming down the hall, about two o'clock in the morning," he said. "You always heard them, because the night before the enlisted officer read who was on the next day and you knew you were going. So you didn't sleep too soundly. And I can still hear those guys coming down the hall.

"We bombed not in France, but in Belgium, and from there on up, the whole area," he said. "And then we went up in Berlin. That was quite a ride, to go all the way from England to Berlin, carrying a load of bombs. It took a good 10 hours."

Although the maximum limit set for bombing missions started out at 25, it was boosted to 30 before Lawson started flying. Most of his missions were flown over German soil.

"We did go down into the lower end, down into Czechoslovakia," he said. "Of course, Dresden and all that, that's on the lower end of Germany. Railroads were the predominant thing at that time, and bridges. The Bulge was just over with and of course they wanted to try and trap the German forces."

His crew tried over and over to knock out the Hohenzollern bridge in Cologne, even dropping Navy depth charges in the river, but couldn't remove it. They hit the bridge, but it was built so well it would not collapse.

"But the thing we're proud of is there's a magnificent cathedral there at the Hohenzollern bridge, and we never touched it," he said. "Those guys knew what they were doing. They were good bombardiers, good crews."

George was held at Moosburg for nearly a year. During that time, he had plenty of time to study human nature and the enemy he'd only known in the skies.

"The German people in general were apathetic towards any revenge," he said. "They were not vicious-oriented, such as some of the SS troops were — they lived on it. It was their main purpose in life, I think, some of them."

The camp was liberated in May of 1945 and the prisoners were taken to France and then sent home. He was discharged in January 1946.

"I was a rookie," he said. "There were, particularly the English, and some Americans in there four, five years. And they still were lucky compared to the fellows in the Far East — they really caught it, health-wise and everything else. If you can be happy about something, I was always happy that I was where I was instead of over on that side."

The Precious Link To Home

Mail comforted GIs and families

Imagine being far away, in France or Italy or Africa. It's 1943 or '44. After days on rocky hillsides or in an Army hospital you'd receive a letter from home. To hear from someone you loved in a world gone mad might be the only stable aspect of your life.

Taking time to sit down and write to someone far away served not only as a means of communication — it was also a comfort to both the writer and recipient, on both sides of the oceans.

Local veterans of World War II and their families have shared letters that they wrote and were sent at that time.

South Luzon, Philippines
Batangas
Dec. 9, 1945

Dear Mom,
Received your letters of Nov. 25 and 27 today and Ken's address sounds right. I know about where he is. He is also a truck driver. Maybe I'll meet him somewhere. As you know I am on the road a lot.

I have 3 years in this month, a hash mark. It doesn't seem possible I have been gone so long.

The 14th A.A.C. means 14th Anti Aircraft Command. It's the command in the south part of the island. There are really some beautiful places around here.

Am glad you received the rifle. They were taken from the Japanese near here but I didn't take them personally. I did get some uniforms from a captain myself.

It isn't yet cold here, just damp and a little uncomfortable. All in all the weather is fair.

I went to Church today and I try hard to go every Sunday. Next Sunday the new Chapel will be dedicated and I'd like very much to go. The chaplain is very good.

I am going to write to Ken and tell him where I am. I hope we can meet.

Be good and be careful and take care of things.

Your loving son,
"Dick"

Letters were the only connection to home for soldiers during World War II. Pictured above is an envelope dated August 2, 1945, a piece of photocopied 'V-mail', and a 1944 service photograph of Richard Wood.

For Richard Wood of Oneonta, this is part of the way it was. A private first class in the 389th Anti-Aircraft Artillery Automatic Weapons Battalion in the Philippines during World War II, he was trained to be a driver and anti-aircraft relay man from 1942 to early 1946. He wrote letters back home to Oneonta, usually at least once a week. Mostly he wrote to his aunt and guardian, Ruth Graves, whom he called "Mom," or his father, William Wood.

Veterans' letters varied in the amount they revealed about what was actually happening in the war. Army censors sometimes deleted information that could have helped the Germans or Japanese had it fallen into their hands. Marshall Smith of Otego remembers stringent mail rules from his Navy days from 1943 to '46.

"Every letter that was written by us was censored before it left the ship," Smith said. "Every officer would censor the letters of his men. In the beginning, they cut words out with scissors, if there were things you couldn't write about. You couldn't write about the weather, or the time of day, and never where you were. You couldn't even tell them what country you were in. Later they just blacked it out.

"You weren't allowed to discharge garbage from the ship, because dates would be on letters and if the Germans found letters with dates on them they'd wait for convoys and torpedo you," he said.

V-mail, or Victory mail, was created with a new technology.

"V-mail was something when Xeroxing was just a new thing," Smith said. "They'd take a letter

Dick Wood sits in the kitchen of his home on Oneida Street in Oneonta, surrounded by letters he wrote home during World War II. (Photo by Julie Lewis)

"We had alerts many times, at 2 or 3 in the morning. They'd sight an unidentified plane and give us a red alert. They'd say, 'Take your clothes and run.' We'd run down there in our underwear and get dressed. Then you had to stay there until they were identified, maybe an hour, an hour and a half.

"But there were no sirens, or anything like that. It was just us that knew it; people in the city never knew it," he said.

Wood was part of the 769th Anti-Aircraft Battalion in San Diego, and was part of the first anti-aircraft outfit to be trained as a rocket battalion.

"The rockets were in a cluster, with a lot more firepower," he said. "It wasn't just a shell that hit the airplane. It would explode when it hit the target."

After being trained to use rockets in Oklahoma, Wood was shipped out to the Philippines and landed on the island of Luzon at the Lingayan Gulf near San Fabian.

Luzon, Philippines
July 18, 1945

Dearest Mom,
Just to let you know everything is going along fine and no need for worry. Have been working just about all day long today. I traded some cigarettes for a few bananas. A good deal. Last night I went down to the creek and took a bath and washed some clothes. Don't forget to send some stationery and stamps. They are scarce around here.

It's getting dark so I'll have to quit. Say hello to all and be good. I hope Bob will be able to take care of the car for his use.

Your loving son,
"Dick"

and it was photocopied, and they cut it down so the letter was maybe five inches by six inches. Everything was shrunk; it was just to save space and weight on the ships and the planes, since mail was the last priority. A lot of times they'd push the rice paper too, to save weight. It was so light and thin you didn't even know you were holding a paper in your hand."

In addition to being in the Philippines, Richard Wood also wrote home from California, where he was sent to protect the coast in 1942 and '43, before being moved to the Pacific.

"We had our guns set up in the streets in San Diego, right in the city, waiting for the Japanese to attack," Wood said. "They were 90 millimeter, 3 1/2-inch guns, with four to a battery. The shells weighed 42 pounds apiece.

Some letters from Donald Lingner of Oneonta are in a scrapbook held by Richard Rose, Laurens town historian. Lingner spent 1942-1945 stationed in Belgium, France and Germany in the Army Air Corps as a technical sergeant, working on planes. He wrote to his aunt, Hazel Wright of Oneonta, and his grandmother, Hattie Wright. Like Dick Wood, Lingner maintained a mostly-light note in his letters home.

Oct. 17, 1944
Belgium

Dear Grandmother,
It is about time I wrote to you. How have you been, I have been just fine. Thanks a lot for the box you sent me it was sure swell, just what I needed.

The people over here are OK but you have to watch them. I have been to Paris and to Reims. When I get a chance I am going to Brussels. The cities over here are very clean. Wish I could tell you more but I cannot. It will have to wait until I get home, which I hope is soon. Am getting pretty tired of this kind of life.

... Have Aunt Mildred and Frank been out lately. Sure would like to see all of the folks back home. Miss you all like the devil.

Well Grandma I have got to close for now as much as I hate to. God bless you.

Loads of love,
Don

Minnie Darling was another Oneontan who wrote to Hazel Wright, since they both belonged to the Monday Bowling League in Oneonta. As a member of the Women's Army Auxiliary Corps stationed in Hobbs, N.M., she worked in the public relations office as a bond clerk. Darling's letters exude the excitement that civilians were sometimes shown in newsreels, as the first letter indicates. Another letter from Minnie Darling to Hazel Wright gives the flavor of being in the service across the states at Christmastime.

Fort Oglethorpe, Georgia
4/17/43

Dear Bowlers,

*So much has happened since I last saw "you all" that I don't know where to begin. The most important thing just happened this morning. Our company was chosen as honor escort for President Roosevelt. He reviewed us also in a parade of the whole post — we're the **first** WAAC post to be reviewed by the President and we sure did strut our stuff.*

They took movies of the escort and parade — so watch for it and maybe you'll see us. Most of us have only been here about 10 days and we have been drilled 'till we're ready to drop, but we all love it.

We have classes, tests, drills, "shots" in the arm etc., in our basic training now and in about 2 weeks I hope to be sent to Officer's Training.

...I'm still so thrilled from seeing and greeting the President that I doubt this letter will make sense but you know me — always nuts anyhow — sooooo write me, everybody and I'll get a card to you sometime.

My address
Aux. Minnie Darling
Co. 2-22 Regt.
3rd WAAC TC
Ft. Oglethorpe, Ga.

29 Dec. '43
Hobbs, New Mexico

Dear Hazel:

Gosh, it sure seemed good to hear from you and right now I'm smelling mighty nice from the soap you gave me. (I'm on duty tonite as B.P. in our dayroom & am interrupted so often I can't keep my mind on this letter.)...

I wrote the script for a Christmas radio show on Christmas nite which was broadcast from 7:30-8 p.m. in Hobbs. Then we all came back to the base & piled into a big open truck with a portable organ & sang Christmas carols all over the post. We almost froze but about 30 WACs & GIs piled out of the truck and were fed coffee & fruitcake in our dayroom — and we're going to go on a straw ride later and repeat the singing...

Sorry you've been not up to par. Better come in the WACs & get built up. They sure need expert typists. I just can't seem to connect you with potatoes — but then things have changed — haven't they?

Take care of yourself & don't try to do so darn much. Give everyone my love & keep a heap for you.

Thanx again
Minnie

Letters prove love could face any obstacle

With so many people apart overseas, there were bound to be thousands of love letters. Richard Bingham of Warnerville has letters from his stepfather, Robert Foley, who served in the army from 1940 to 1946. Foley saved the letters from his first wife, Eleanor, who died in 1959.

The couple was married in February of 1943. This letter from Eleanor to Robert was written about a month before their wedding:

Friday
Jan. 15, 1943

Dearest Bob,

My past couple letters have been quite short, but maybe this will be longer. I'll write small.

... There is something about having either a husband or wife which gives a person a much fuller life. A man and a woman belong together and when two people decide to join their lives it seems they both have a more successful life. Never heard of a successful man that was a bachelor or vice versa. It certainly gives life a lot more meaning, doesn't it.

I do look forward to the time when we will be together. It does make time drag, but keep your hope up and work ahead. I have an idea there are some very fine things in store for you and I. More than we have any idea. Also feel you are going to make out fine in the army.

Remember the day you registered? We took our supper out to North Park. Afterwards we were just talking and I remember saying to you I felt that my life would be more than just the ordinary — something rather colorful and different. You said you felt that way too. Now it seems to me even more so that we are going to that goal. I know you understand now as you did then. It is like something exciting is running right below the surface. Do you feel that?

Last night at Trinity I saw your name in one of the frames. On the right (there in the church) is a list of the fellows from the diocese in the service with a small table in front which always is set with white flowers and candles. It was nice to see your name there. Makes me feel like I really belong.

I like the word "cherish" too. If a couple does that, they don't have to worry about the word "obey."

... We had a black out last night. We were caught at church and had to go to the basement. It was just like the pictures you see in England. I was worried about Dad, since he couldn't hear it, but the warden came down and told him so it worked out all right. We probably will be away when the next one comes.

Will write more later.

Love,
Eleanor

Three months after their wedding this letter from him reads:

May 1, 1943
APO 8882
c/o Postmaster N.Y.

Darling Wife,
It is now 12 midnight and I am just getting around to writing you Dearest. We are very busy organizing and have little time to write. Longer letters when I have time.

We have a fine group of officers here and things are coming along fine. The officers that came on the train have had to start from scratch and organize ourselves from the ground up. So we are doing 10 things at once.

I am in charge of a platoon and we pretty well manage things ourselves in the Co...

Darling, I love you very much. A person never realizes to the fullest extent how much until it is impossible to see them again.

Dearest, I can not give you whys & wherefores. If I did it would wind up as Military information. But here are the facts. It will be impossible for you to visit me. I cannot tell you my whereabouts.

I may be able to telephone, I will try to. I can't say when I am leaving. Don't be alarmed if I don't write for some time. Don't worry about me. Keep yourself healthy & don't try to save too much money. Don't work unless you wish to. I shall not be able to see you for a long time. But I shall think of you all the time and look toward that happy day when I shall see my own wife again. Until then Darling take care of yourself and your Dad.

... We have so many happy memories kid, I reckon I can live on them for quite some time. Write as often as you can. All my love & devotion to a wonderful wife.
Your best Husband,
Bob

Robert also addressed Eleanor as "Murph" in some letters, probably based on her maiden name, Murray.

July 22, 1943
Thursday
No. 3

Darling Murph,
Received two beautiful letters from you this evening. Sure was happy to receive them. Makes the whole day worth while. I certainly hope you are getting all my letters for I write every day.

And when I must work too much and can't write that day I double the next day's output.

I am well Darling and living good.

My job here at this place as Mess Officer will be over soon, thank the Lord. I can eat the meals all right but I sure don't care for all the problems that go with getting the men fed. It's not like home, I can tell you.

The one problem I can't lick is the division of meat. No matter how I do it the business is pure guess work. You see we don't get so many small units. They send us two or three sides to make our total strength and we cut it down for each Co.

No tools either, we use a carpenter's saw and a knife. Certainly will be glad when this duty comes to an end. We get relieved this next week end and I shall be so glad. It's been a mighty tough job. Lezette says I am beginning to talk in my sleep.

You asked me which girl reminds me of you. Well Dear, you are in a class by yourself. I'd say they both remind me of you, perhaps the girl he married a bit more so. But that could be because she was more in the picture. You occupy the entire picture to me.

You're such an illogical little monkey dearest. Here you don't want me to come home in the middle of the night 'cause you might be wearing blue pajamas.

I sure don't catch the difference. If you think that should I get home at midnight by chance and pound the pavement till daybreak you are absolutely crazy.

Darling you could be clad in an old potato sack for all I care. It's you I'm interested in seeing. Anyhow what's wrong with the all blue pajamas. They looked all right to me, what I saw of them.

Darling it will sure be one happy day for me when I see you again. And I don't care if it's morning, noon or night. It's all the same to me, as you'll no doubt find out. Can't help thinking what a lucky girl you are. (Fooled you that time.)

Can't get you out of my mind and sure don't want to. But I must close dear and will with all my love and devotion.

You are sweeter by far than honey. Your husband loves you and how.

Love & kisses to the Blonde.
 Your best husband,
 Bob

Robert Foley spent time in North Africa serving alongside the British, as well as in General George Patton's Fifth Army in Italy, and elsewhere in Europe. He was a company commander, and was promoted to captain.

"He told me a lot about what he'd been through and what he'd done," Bingham said. "He was wounded three times; he spent a good amount of time in the hospital."

Sunday, April 29, 1945

Dearest Bob,

How are you? Hope you are safe. The radios give us quite a bit of information about the Fifth Army. My one consolation is that you will be in on the finish now. I wish you were home, but guess if you were and your army defeated all the Germans you would have a little feeling inside that you wish you would have been there for the end.

Yesterday afternoon and evening I washed the paints, windows and curtains in our room just in case you get home this next month.

Mother called in the evening. They had heard Germany surrendered. It was a false report.

I have been interested in the San Francisco conference. Russia has some different ideas, but they seem to be doing a good job in compromising. Last night I heard a commentator say the man to watch is John Ford. He appears to be the speaker for the little nations.

How I want you home. Am not getting my hopes up. But do plan how it will be. There is a chance. I don't know what to think, though, since the offensive. Will that make a difference in rotation?

Darling, we can have a wonderful time. It will be warm enough for picnics. How grand it will be to walk around out in the open. Eat over a fire and sleep under the stars. I guess none of this will be new to you. But we will surely have fun.

It is quite late now. I saved this bit until I went to bed. Feel very close to you tonight. I was reading sometime between 9 and 9:30 and suddenly I felt you come into the room. Darling I pray you are all right. I cannot picture a life without you. Your return and our future together means more than anything in the world. We have been closer in our short time together than many couples ever are in a lifetime. I love you so completely. You have been a most wonderful husband. I probably have these silly fears tonight because the end is so close. But I know you will be back, and it might be within this month.

All my love to my dearest husband,
 Eleanor

Family learns of father's past through letters

Arthur L. Tyler in Italy, circa 1945.

As well as providing glimpses into parts of their daily lives, some veterans reflected in letters on the nature of war, their enemies — and government. One man who wrote a good deal on those topics was Arthur L. Tyler, in letters to his mother, Jeanette, at home in Teaneck, N.J.

Janice Armstrong of Delhi, his daughter, now has those letters but not many details of her father's role in the war. She was a toddler then, born in 1941.

All she knows is that he served as an Army private, was promoted to sergeant, and that his letters were written from June 1944 to August 1946. He was in a non-combat unit in Italy, part of the time in the occupation.

"He never talked about it — that was strictly off limits," Armstrong said. "It's possible that he talked with someone else about it, like my grandfather, but whenever I asked him about it he brushed me off."

His letters speak for themselves.

Naples, Italy
25 July 1945
Wed. 4 p.m.

Dearest Mom & all,
... It's a funny thing but when the fighting is over even your enemy seems to look different. I say this because you mentioned about the Americans talking and being somewhat friendly with the Germans. I still hate them and the Italians too but when war is over and the two foes are thrown together there is bound to be some letdown in the hatred.

Being in a strange country where there are little children and pretty girls (I imagine there are some in Germany) some GIs can't help feeling lonely for something other than army life and war. It's hard to see a cute baby (don't even have to be cute) and not feel a pang of sympathy in your heart. To any soldier who has children it brings thoughts and memories of home so he just can't help making some exception to his hatred.

Even the tough and hard hearted soldier has a soft spot in his heart and when the fighting is over he forgets his tension and turns toward something that takes his mind off of what he's been through. I'm not trying to convince you that any of our boys should open their arms and hearts to the Germans but even as much as I hate these two faced Italians there are times when I forget and almost forgive.

Men go crazy and kill in battle but after it is all over he forgets and wants to act human again. I don't even like working with the

Germans or the Italians but I have to and tolerate them. Even so, when they are with you day after day you sometimes relax your hate and find yourself doing something out of the way. I can't hate 24 hours a day, and neither can others. It just isn't in our blood or is it our way of life. I read and hear hate all day and am sick and tired of it. Why can't everybody be the same way.

... Your loving son,
Arthur

Here is another one from Arthur L. Tyler, written about three weeks later.

Janice Armstrong (Photo by Sandra Fentiman)

Naples, Italy
18 Aug. 1945
Sat. 5 p.m.

Hello Mom & all,
What a hectic three days this has been! With the announcement of Japan's acceptance of the surrender terms things have been popping right and left. Thurs. afternoon orders were issued to strip a ship (of all equipment) that is loaded with incendiaries and T.N.T. The reason was that it will be towed out to sea and sunk — ship & cargo together. ...We had to take all usable equipment off the ship. All that was left in or on her were bombs. Seems to me that with the so called shortage of shipping space (and ships) other arrangements could be made. That ship could have been reconverted to a troopship. I know there are lots of guys — including me — that would gladly go home on it, no matter how bad the conditions were aboard.

Now here is a big laugh. The gov't. has announced that it has overseas & in the states an oversupply of sheets, pillowcases, towels, razor blades, soap, machines (all kinds), and lots of other stuff similar, so the civilians are to be given the privilege of buying it. No mention has been (or will be) made of giving service men first choice. Boy does our gov't. & its lousy grafters want to make a nice juicy profit. We haven't seen mattresses or sheets since we left

home yet the gov't. gives this stuff to the poor starving Italians. We have a hell of a time getting clothes exchanged yet every damn Italian and German P.W. has a set of GI uniforms— new ones. ...I could go on and on telling what I've seen and know but it would no doubt bore you besides taking hundreds of pages to describe. What an unpleasant stink this all adds up to. Because all these countries get free service I and the rest of the millions of Americans have to pay through the nose. Phooey!

... Well I guess this is all the dirt from this side of the ocean. The way the work is going we don't know what's next. The sooner it gets done the sooner we get home. That shouldn't be too far away now.

Lots of love to my only Mom, Dad and brother and plenty of kisses too. Bye for now.

Your loving son,
Arthur

Armstrong said her father kept the letters in his attic for many years.

"My father was a pack rat," she said. "I think, too, maybe he wanted to be reminded of that time once in a while."

Though Tyler died in 1988, Armstrong said the war memorabilia is something she wants to pass on to her children.

"My son has a scrapbook and a World War II pistol of my father's," she said.

War Splits Families For The Holidays

Schenevus man recalls his first Christmas alone

Hal Winter at the border between the United States and Canada in 1945.

Like many sailors, Hal Winter of Schenevus couldn't make it home for the holidays during World War II. Stationed in Little Creek, Va., Christmas 1942 was his first away from home, and he was homesick.

"It was depressing. Everybody else seemed to be getting leave, and the Little Creek boat crews were not getting leave, we were kept on the base," he said. "I tried to get to the phone to call home, and the line was so long I just gave up on Christmas Eve.

"Every time I went out into the open air I saw new Christmas decorations on the telephone poles and I said, 'The hell with this' and I would turn my back on it. I wasn't bitter about that, I was just bitter about being in the amphibious force. It was the biggest disappointment of my life."

Although he wanted duty on a destroyer, the Navy switched Winter to the amphibious forces, where he became a "bowhook." He was aboard the USS *Calvert*, an attack transport ship, which was nearly 500 feet long. But he transported troops onto Pacific islands on a ramp boat that held 36 troops.

"I had to sit up forward in the boat with a long pole with a hook on it," he said. "I would have to grab the lines when we were coming alongside the ship, so we could become attached to the ship after we were finished dumping our soldiers or marines onto the beach."

"Yes, I was homesick at Christmastime. We were very, very busy and always very tired, but there were moments, especially around the holidays, when you felt it.

"I took a walk on Christmas Day night, in the fog, and I sort of lost myself in that fog and tried to take an accounting of myself. I was 20, and I tried to assess myself on this long, introspective walk, and I decided not to let myself get depressed so easily. That was a big improvement for me at that age," he said.

The following year, he was in Hawaii and went back to San Diego near the holidays.

"I felt so far away from home in Little Creek, because it was so near and yet so far," Winter said. "I'm from Hempstead, Long Island. I was a Yankee, a New Yorker. In San Diego, 3100 miles away from home, I didn't feel too badly because I knew damn well I would never be able to make it home unless they gave me a lengthy leave."

In 1944, Winter's ship was anchored in the Admiralty Islands in the South Pacific at Christmastime. It seemed to him as if all the entertainment the guys had on the ship was old, bad movies. So he decided to put on a theatrical show complete with harmonicas, banjos, guitars and costumes.

These are handmade Christmas cards that Hal Winter of Schenevus created for his parents while he served during World War II. He spent his first year away from home at Christmas while in the U.S. Navy.

"By that time we were all pretty fed up with the war," he said. "We'd gone through several stages. We had arrived there from New Guinea on the 16th of December. And by this time we had been through several invasions, by the way. There was Tarawa, Makin, and there was Kwajalein, and there was Leyte, which was the Philippines. That's when MacArthur went ashore, and got his pants wet. I think after that we went to Saipan."

"So I got two or three of my shipmates to help me make grass skirts and cardboard bras and I got them to rehearse a dance with me," he said. "We did all this in secrecy; nobody knew about it except the three of us. It was supposed to be a big surprise. And come the night of the show, these two guys pooped out they would not do it. So I got up there and did my own hula and brought the house down."

Winter wasn't normally homesick at sea; it would only strike him occasionally. In spite of the war, he saw being in the Navy as an adventure, and a chance to be independent of his parents. Still, it wasn't all stage shows.

"We were under fire a lot. It wasn't one of those things where you never saw action," he said. "We were under fire at Sicily. We brought troops into the shore at Sicily under the glare of the enemy parachute lights. They would send up rockets, because we were invading at 3 o'clock in the morning and it was still dark. Another time we were bombed and strafed on the beach. So that was scary. I thought I was going to be a coward and turn tail, but there was no place to run to."

"In between all of this invasion business, we were bouncing back and forth from island to island that had already been taken because these lagoons were used as jumping off places, staging areas for the next invasion. Also for refueling, although there were times when we did refuel at sea. And we also got to go ashore on one of the little islands for beer parties.

"There were no natives, but lots of little native huts but the officers had all that," Winter said. "We had the open fields where we played baseball under hot, blistering sun. We would go for one day and come back around 4 or 5 o'clock in the afternoon. Whenever we came back from an invasion we were usually given a day or two of that kind of liberty, if it was available to us and to the skipper. If he had pull anywhere, his ship would get called into port."

After the invasion of Makin in November of '43, Winter became a quartermaster, involved in navigation of the same ship, but more removed from the physical invasion. But no matter what his job was, he never let on to his family in letters the homesickness he felt from time to time.

One thing he did do was make Christmas cards to send home.

"I tried to do something different every year," he said. "I went out and bought colored ink in Honolulu. I tried to make my parents feel good by sending them some handmade artwork, you know. I tried to make them proud of me."

Spending Christmas Behind Enemy Lines

As a girl, Oneonta woman was trapped in Nazi-occupied Belgium

Betty Laitsch, 11, in Nazi-occupied Belgium.

Fifty years ago, World War II not only kept soldiers and sailors from home for the holidays, it separated people caught in the line of fire. For Betty Laitsch of Oneonta, Christmases were spent trapped in a country oppressed by the Nazis.

Laitsch is an American born to a Belgian mother and French father. In 1939 she and her sister were taken to Charleroi, Belgium, to attend school and live with relatives. They ended up stranded there until 1946.

"I went over with my mother," Laitsch said, at her home on Southside Drive. "She was sick, but she wanted me to meet the family. We had only one passport then; she registered me, but she took the passport back with her. That's how it was done then."

Just 10 years old, Laitsch started school, and when war broke out in Europe in September 1939, Belgium and the Netherlands declared neutrality. In May 1940 Belgians' peaceful lives were shattered when Adolf Hitler sent in his troops.

"At the time when the Germans came through on May 10, there was no more communication," Laitsch said. "That was it. My parents couldn't send money. Naturally, my mother was very worried, because the Germans had a very bad reputation from 1914 — the first World War."

When the Germans invaded, Laitsch remembers her grandmother came to get her at school, an hour's drive from her home. They boarded a train to France, in an effort to reach relatives in Paris. But after several hours on the train, it stopped, unable to continue. French troops were blowing up bridges to stop the Germans' march.

"So we decided to walk to France," she said. "Everybody was trying to escape; we took what we could carry. And my grandmother was in her 70s, so it was kind of slow going along.

"I remember walking at night. People would pick us up in carts and give us a ride — there were no cars," she said. Sleeping in a field and eating moldy bread, they were into France on the second day of walking when their hopes were crushed — by the sound of motor vehicles.

"We heard this noise behind us and it was the Germans, coming behind us on the road," she

Betty Laitsch of Oneonta stands with her husband, John, holding a jacket covered with military patches that she began collecting when Belgium was liberated by the Allies. (Photo by Julie Lewis)

"They were very precise; I had to be there at 10 o'clock, if I remember right," she said. "I signed my name for the officers in uniform, and left."

The Charleroi area was home to about 100,000 people, and she was restricted to a 25-square kilometer area around it. The German presence was now felt everywhere.

"There were big flags hung from buildings, and signs in German on the street," Laitsch said. "We had to obey their rules completely. Food was a big problem. The winter of '42 was the worst; there was very little food. They gave us stamps, and we could get a certain amount."

She had a French cousin named Roger Lignieres, who was 18 years older than she. He was a French citizen who had lived with them before the invasion. He joined the French army when France went to war; later he suddenly appeared.

"One day he knocked on my grandmother's door. We hadn't seen him in months," Laitsch said. "He was the only breadwinner we had, and he went back to his job; he was a brewmaster. And he was the only male in the house."

Still, there was no contact with her parents.

"I missed my mother, and I cried at times. But I was with the family and there were so many things to do," Laitsch said. "They don't have a Christmas like we do; it was celebrated as a religious holiday.

said. "And they were coming through, telling everyone to get off the roads and go home." As troops passed them by on the way to Paris, they all knew there was now nowhere to go — except home. So they had to go back the way they came.

After that, Laitsch's life went on in a different way. She still went to school, but for the next few years had to report once a week to Nazi headquarters. She had no papers, so they wanted to keep track of her.

"In Belgium, the night of Dec. 5 Saint Nicholas comes. Usually what we'd do is put wooden shoes or a plate out with a carrot or something, and he'd replace it with a treat like chocolate. Even in school, every child got a chocolate bar that day — even during the war. I don't know how they did that."

In order to get by, people were creative. They made clothes from tablecloths and warmed wine with herbs for supper. Teen-age boys would climb onto trains to open doors and allow coal and wood to spill from cars. Residents waited quietly by the tracks and filled up burlap bags with the fuel.

There were other changes, too. Jewish people in the city had to wear yellow stars. And there were Russian prisoners held at a camp, who were forced to march to work in coal mines. Laitsch knew where prisoners were sometimes executed by firing squad.

Betty Laitsch, 16, ready to leave Belgium.

"The Russians were guarded; we could see them walking sometimes," she said. "What we used to do as kids was we'd walk by and throw apples over the wall to them. Belgium had a lot of fruit."

In September of '44 her sector was liberated by the Allies. Laitsch was now 15. Christmas-time that year brought her new independence and excitement — and a man she would marry 43 years later.

"Around Christmas was when I started working at the Quartermaster Depot. Since I could speak English and French, I got this nice, paying job. And I could bring Belgian francs back to my aunt; it was great."

John Laitsch from Milwaukee was in the Army Quartermaster Corps. The depot was like a warehouse, with food, clothing and supplies to be distributed.

"I had been in France and I moved up to Charleroi, and was attached there for three or four months," he said. "I was assigned to the headquarters and was working out of there and I heard this American voice, female, and I thought, 'What the heck?' So I went and talked to her."

The couple decided they liked each other, but she was too young to date. So John took his weekly carton ration of cigarettes to Betty's aunt, who then reconsidered her rule.

John was in the service until April of '46, after signing up for two extra 90-day stints in order to stay with Betty in Belgium. Betty's parents lived in New York City, and she returned in November that year.

"After he got back we were writing letters. We wrote for quite a while," Betty said. "And then he told me he was getting married. He broke my heart."

Later Betty also married. They wrote annual Christmas cards, but she and John didn't meet again until 1987.

"After Betty's husband died, she came to visit, and my wife died a year later," John said. "So we decided to get back together." And they were married in 1989.

Children saved tin foil that was wrapped around their chewing gum. All metal scraps at home were saved for making bombs. Fat trimmed from scarce cuts of meat was saved and rendered for the cause. It was World War II on the home front.

Some local people remember those days and the sacrifices made by almost everyone. Mary Buck of Colliersville was a registered nurse still in her teens when the war broke out. At the time, she lived with her parents on Staten Island.

"I worked at Halloran General Hospital as a civilian nurse," she said. "It was actually being built as a school and in 1940 was still just in its beginnings. It was more or less grabbed up to be used by the military. Everything stopped being 'normal' and went toward the war effort. It later became Willowbrook State School."

Buck noted that women's roles were different then, too. It was a "big thing" for women to go outside their own community, or to work at a paying job.

"My mother absolutely forbid us to be in the service," she said. "She thought it was unladylike to go into the military. But it was quite a glamorous thing — you wanted to be part of the action, to make it work. There was a great patriotism in those days."

That patriotic feeling may have been what helped America succeed. Rosalyn Niles of Oneonta was born in 1941, and has early memories of playing with ration stamps after the war and hearing her parents talk.

"My earliest recollection is going down to the rail station by where L. P. Butts is now and seeing big boxes unloaded from the train," Niles said. "The train would pull up there and its doors would slide back and boxes draped with American flags would be slid out."

That was in 1946.

"In those days, children were seen and not heard," she said at her West Street home. "Your mother took you by the hand — there were no baby sitters. You were told, 'Just behave.' The trains came and the doors opened and people were crying.

"I don't remember knowing at the time that they were bodies," she continued. "They were put on wooden wagons, like hay wagons, and tied with ropes."

The War Effort On The Home Front

Area people recall sacrifices made during WWII

From all that she's heard, Niles doesn't believe there was anyone untouched by the war.

"Every single day there was the radio, the news of the war," she said. "Just getting your gas revolved around the war."

Buck agreed. Walking down the street, dark blue flags with a gold star were visible in window panes, indicating that a son or husband had died in the war effort.

"Your heart would just go out to these people," she said.

Food rationing was also ever-present.

"My mother had the most difficulty getting sugar and butter — those few people who had cars might have wanted to trade for gasoline rations," she said. "Don't forget, we came through the De-pression, so we knew how to do without. Today, I think if we had rationing, people would be weeping and moaning.

"They didn't hesitate to tighten their belts and pull up their boots and help out. Even if they'd already done their share, they'd do some more," she continued.

There were times when people became depressed, Buck said, by news of the war, or their personal losses. But you were expected to forget peace-time behavior and pitch in to help where you could.

"I never heard anybody complain," she said. "They were positive we would win."

There was a fear that America would be attacked from the air and precautions were taken at night, Niles remembers.

Mary Buck of Colliersville looks over a scrapbook with news clippings of Oneonta people in World War II, along with ration coupons and newspapers from the war years. (Photo by Julie Lewis)

"There were sirens in Oneonta, and most of the time they were drills," she said. "When the sirens went off, everybody turned off the lights and pulled their curtains. The street lights went off."

Some residents were designated air raid wardens who walked the streets, checking for lights. But everyone wasn't plunged in total darkness; they could use a Victory light.

"It was just a light bulb that screwed into a socket into a little wooden base," Niles said. "There was a cobalt blue light bulb with a V filament."

Ration coupons from the 1940s.

Niles' mother, Edith Angellotti Kellogg, kept a scrapbook with news clippings of Oneonta people who went away to war. She also kept left-over ration coupons and stamps, and copies of government-issued sugar certificates that were used at Angellotti's Grocery on Fair Street.

Looking over the sugar certificates and the scrapbook reminded Buck how cakes sometimes fared in wartime.

"Someone had a wedding during the war and had one of those elaborate tier cakes," she said. "But it had a gray tone, without any butter or sugar. Everybody was trying to be polite, but it really wasn't edible."

Just because she stayed stateside doesn't mean Buck had no contact with soldiers or prisoners. In fact, she saw plenty of both.

"New patients were coming in all the time, at what is now Newark Airport, from combat areas in Europe," she said. "Men were picked up right in the battlefield and given field assistance, and brought here as soon as possible. We would take the ambulances and go over to the airport, to be there when the plane came in."

Buck isn't a tall woman, and one problem she had was reaching the clutch in the ambulance. At times it made for jerky riding.

"Some of the soldiers joked with me that they'd made it through battle and being wounded, only to die by my hands as a driver," she said. Buck treated soldiers who had been wounded on the Anzio beachhead in Italy — some burned by flame throwers. Many had been hit in the face and required skin grafts to repair their features.

"They would go through such pain," she said. "They did have painkiller; a lot of them were on morphine and a lot would become addicted. But you didn't know what to do. You knew they were in agony because of their wounds."

She and the other nurses also donated blood to the hospital, saw patients with mental breakdowns from wartime trauma, and treated those with venereal disease — before antibiotics were discovered. And if she paused to look out the window, she might see some prisoners at work.

"When Italy fell, some Italian prisoners were brought here and kept in barracks," Buck said. "They were very happy — they had it nicer at the hospital than other places. They used them working the grounds and cleaning. There was usually one military person watching them. But they weren't under lock and key."

On A Wing And A Prayer

Oneonta man recounts day he fought Japanese Zeros and death

The Sunday morning dawned clear and bright. Setting out on a routine mission from New Georgia Island in the South Pacific, Oneonta native Samuel Bertuzzi didn't know that September 14, 1943 would be a day he would never forget.

Navy flyer Bertuzzi had been in the Pacific since 1941. Fifty years ago, at the height of World War II, fighting in the Pacific was fierce and had been for months.

Day after day the lieutenant flew missions against Japanese targets. But Sept. 14 was different, and he hasn't forgotten a detail.

That morning, when the Oneonta man took his place in a group of 18 Grumman Hellcats, his target was a Japanese airstrip roughly 150 miles northwest — Ballale, in the Solomon Islands.

After reaching its target, the squadron was attacked by 60 Japanese Zero fighters. After Bertuzzi shot down one Zero, three others surrounded his plane. A 90 mm shell smashed through the right side of his Hellcat, exploding into the cockpit and shattering his right arm as well as the communications and instrument panel.

"The panic was just incredible," he said. "I thought, 'Christ, I'm going to die.' What can I do? What can I do?'

"Of course my first impulse was to bail out. The plane wasn't burning, or anything else, but my arm was all shattered, and my leg, so I knew that I couldn't fly.

"The hood was controlled by a crank that was up on the right-hand side," he said, reaching forward in his chair as if to turn it. "You had to do it with your right hand; if you cranked it back, it came off. There was an emergency release that you could use, but I couldn't reach it with my left hand."

By this time the dogfight was miraculously over — the other planes had disappeared, both his squadron and the Zeros.

"So all of a sudden I calmed down," he said. "I knew I couldn't get out. If I had bailed out, I probably would have landed with the Japanese and been killed anyway. So I thought I had to try to fly back.

"At that point I could see no other plane in the whole sky. Evidently I had fallen off to the side," he continued. "All the instruments were gone, nothing there. The only thing that was working was the motor, thank God. And I looked down in the bottom of the cockpit and it was just covered with my blood. And I kept thinking I was going to bleed to death. And I almost did."

After a while his bleeding slowed down.

"Later on I found out that sometimes the shells, when they explode, have a little bit of powder that acts like a cauterizing agent," Bertuzzi said.

But he had no idea where he was going now.

"The only thing I could do was look at the sun and fly south, southeast, so it's got to be over my left shoulder. There are so many islands, my God. Here and here and here," he said, pointing.

"By that point I had calmed down enough so I knew approximately how far I had to fly, if I could find the landing field."

At home on Clinton Street in Oneonta, Samuel Bertuzzi wears his Navy dress blue uniform from World War II. He holds a photo of himself taken after being wounded in the South Pacific. (Photo by Julie Lewis)

So Bertuzzi flew toward what he hoped would be his base.

"The only place of protection, so to speak, when you're out over the water is to fly right on the water, then of course if a plane tries to attack then it can't come down because then it would go in.

"All of a sudden I see these tracers go by — tracers are bullets. And I look back and here are two Zeros chasing me. And one of them just creased this shoulder," he said, pointing up to his left. "Thank God it didn't knock my left arm out, because that was the only thing I had to fly with."

Desperately he starting "jinking" the plane from left to right as he flew, making it hard for his pursuers to hit him.

"The good old Grumman motor kept going and going," he said. "I was looking back and they would try to raise up to get a run on me, but as they would raise up they'd lose a little speed and I'd pull away. And after about 50 miles they gave up. Now I have absolutely no idea where I am."

All of a sudden he saw another plane, following him off to one side.

"Then I could see it was one of ours. And who was it? It was my wing man. And after it was all overwith and I got talking with him I said, 'How the hell did you ever find me? I looked around and I couldn't see anybody.' And he said, 'Sam, I looked off as we were finally regrouping and starting back. I looked out and I saw a little glint on the water. I knew you got hit, so I came over and there you were.' "

After putting his wrist up to his forehead, the signal that he was hurt, Bertuzzi followed his flying partner to the base.

"Now he was a little confused at this point. So where does he lead me but 200 feet right over a Japanese airfield! At least at that point, I knew where we were because this field was on an island only about five miles from where we were. And I looked down and there were these Japanese gunners looking up, saying who are these dumb dodos flying over here? So they never even opened up — they were so surprised," he said.

Though he was almost safe as he neared home turf, Bertuzzi had another crisis coming. A plane had crashed on the landing field, and Bertuzzi's landing gear wouldn't come down. A metal matting was used on top of the fields for support, but to land a plane on its belly on the matting could spark an explosion.

"The only alternative I had was to land in the water next to the field, as close as I could," he said. "And finally, after working the lever, I can still feel my finger being all cut, trying to release this emergency mechanism.

"And finally just before coming in to land in the water, the mechanism worked and the canopy went off. So I thought, 'Well geez, I'm not going to drown now.'

"Here again, landing in water, if you don't hit it at the perfect angle, you cartwheel and go over," he said. "But I landed on my belly and I tried to land as close to the landing field as I could because I could see my buddies; they were all out there. When the plane sank, the water was so shallow I could stand up in the cockpit. That was another plus.

"Then they pushed out a rubber boat and they got me and they put me in the boat, and that was the last thing I remember until I woke up in the foxhole in the middle of the night after we'd been shelled. They just tried to patch me up; we were getting bombed and shelled all night long.

"But with all these things, if any one of them hadn't worked out I'd have been a dead duck," he said. "I've got a good crease right here in the top of my shoulder: If it had been a half an inch lower, this arm would have been out."

This was Bertuzzi's second time being wounded in the Pacific. Seven months earlier, in February 1943, he crashed in a Hellcat after running out of gas.

"We were heading for Guadalcanal and I landed in a bunch of coconut trees," he said. He had flown into the sun for five hours and suffered sunstroke as well as a broken jaw, multiple facial cuts and a concussion. Bertuzzi has no memory of that accident — only of waking up in the field hospital later.

He spent about three months in a stateside hospital that time before returning to the Pacific.

Born in Oneonta in 1918, Bertuzzi graduated from Oneonta High School in 1936 and from Middlebury College in 1941. It was August of that year before he joined the Navy.

"Right after the Battle of Midway, they said 'We need some reinforcements' so every one of us that had had a minimal amount of training were being shipped out there," he explained. "I'll never forget when I first got out there, our Pacific fleet was practically nil, we only had one carrier that was still afloat — I think that was the Enterprise. I think if the Japanese had ever realized how weak we were, how annihilated, they would have started invading the West Coast, but thank God they didn't know," he said.

Bertuzzi says he isn't a hero. He was doing his job. After the war, he came back to Oneonta to live. He got married, and had a family, and was postmaster in the city for 32 years, retiring in 1982.

The thing that amazes him now is how much time has passed since that day he was hit.

"No matter if I live to be 150, I guess, the experience would be as vivid as it was then," he said. "I was one of the fortunate few."

When Douglas McKee learned to speak French, he didn't know it would change his life. Not only did the Gilbertsville man get an Army reassignment because he was fluent in French. He lived in France for 36 years after World War II was over.

When he joined the Army in 1942, McKee was 31 years old.

"In '43 after the invasion of North Africa, the U.S. Army thought that everybody in North Africa should speak English, and discovered that not one of them did," he said. "So, suddenly through all the training camps they sent out questionnaires — they were language exams, and everybody who knew a foreign language had to take the exam."

He rated highly on the exam and was chosen for training at military intelligence headquarters in Fort Ritchie, Md.

In January 1944 McKee was sent to England with about 60 other soldiers. The group was divided into teams of six members each in April. McKee's team was first sent to Ireland, where it was attached to the 15th Corps of the U.S. Army. In May it returned to England, outside Oxford, and was still there when the invasion of Normandy took place in June.

McKee and his teammates crossed the English Channel with other members of the 15th Corps about three weeks after D-Day, eventually becoming part of General George Patton's 3rd Army.

"Our job as interpreters was to get all the information about the Germans that we could from the civilian population," he said. "But we didn't do much of any good, because when the breakthrough finally came and the 3rd Army swept out of the Cherbourg peninsula going due south, and then east toward Paris, the Germans retreated so fast and we covered the ground so fast that the civilians couldn't tell us anything. I mean, by the time they told us, we were past that point."

Still, the French population was encouraged to come to the team's mobile headquarters to share what they knew.

"As we went south into Normandy from the peninsula, most of the towns had been destroyed by bombing, by shelling — that kind of thing," McKee said. "You got used to rubble all over the streets; people took to the fields.

Interpreter Served On Different Front

"My teammates were mostly out on the road with their Jeeps and I got stuck in headquarters because there was nobody else in the 15th Corps headquarters who spoke French," he said. "And French people kept turning up and coming in with something to tell."

Once they moved east toward Paris, there was less destruction because the Germans were retreating instead of holding out, he said.

"We were following quite fast," McKee said. "Instead of being in trench warfare, we were jumping in our cars and doing 35 miles or something, before night fell and then we'd park at night and sleep on the ground and the next morning get up and do another 35 miles. It was a very rapid advance after Paris."

After a replacement arrived at headquarters, McKee was finally free to go seek out information with his team. They headed toward Nancy and the foothills of eastern France.

Former Army interpreter Douglas McKee sits in the library of his home in Gilbertsville. (Photo by Julie Lewis)

"There was a pipeline by that time that went from the beaches of Normandy almost to Paris — for fuel for the tanks and for all the vehicles," he said.

"And suddenly all the fuel was requisitioned for the tanks. They had what was called the Red Ball Express, with mostly black drivers. And they were the tanker drivers who kept bringing, all the way from Paris, the fuel so that we could go on."

"We were stopped there, except for the tanks, for about six weeks, during which time the Germans mined the mountains ahead of us. While we were stopped, our team worked with counterintelligence — because counterintelligence was very good at counterintelligence, but they didn't speak French. Their job was to try to catch people who were trying to infiltrate, and we were working with them all through the winter of '44 and '45."

He noted that the Allied counterintelligence groups were in touch with the French state police, or gendarmes.

"No civilians were supposed to be on the roads without an official pass. If they were found on the roads with no papers, no pass, they had to be picked up because there was no way of identifying them. You didn't know if they were French, or German, or French sympathizers with Germans," McKee said.

That became the Corps' main function as it worked its way to Nancy, as well as working with the gendarmes, who didn't speak English.

"That was a very strong Resistance pocket, in the mountains of eastern France," McKee said. "And the Resistance people also helped out a great deal. Naturally if they could round up Germans, they were rounding up Germans but were very tough on them. They were supposed to (turn them in to the corps), but they didn't always; they shot them. The Germans had done such awful things."

"One of the men that we worked with, he and his wife had a farmhouse in that area and they had sheltered a British radioman who was up in the attic, and the Gestapo got them. And the radioman, I think, was killed. And Henri and his wife were taken off to be taken to a concentration camp somewhere.

"But they got away. Henri murdered the sentinel, and they escaped," he said slowly. "He's still alive, I hear from him all the time. I was in touch with them all the years after the war. But he was deeply religious, and murder was on his conscience. So he's been atoning ever since for having killed. But it was either that or the crematorium."

When the Army started moving again it was north through the Saar River Valley.

"Just about 10 miles from the German frontier in the Saar, we wound up in a terrible little town called Saaralbe where we had U.S. counterintelligence, the interpreter team, OSS — that was the elegant, super secret service on our side, they were all Americans. This crummy little town had one hotel, and we took over the hotel and we all lived in it, together sort of all jammed in, and we had an army cook.

"Then suddenly that Ardennes offensive came, and all of our tanks went off to beat it back and we were left and received orders that we had to stay. We had to keep the civilians from getting on the roads and fleeing...We'd had our own armored division, we'd had (French General) Leclerc's armored division and we felt very safe. Then we woke up one morning and there wasn't a tank in sight. So we were left with orders that we could not move, just to keep the civilians reassured.

"We were out all day long, every day, and it was a terrible winter like this one, with snow about three feet deep on the fields," he said. "The gendarmes were stretched along the frontier and hordes of people kept turning up without any identification, no passes or anything, and had to be brought back to be interrogated. They all came back with plausible stories that they'd escaped from prison in Germany and managed to cross the frontier.

"Well, you didn't know who they were. They were Dutch supposedly, Belgians, Frenchmen, maybe Germans, but we had to stop them all," McKee said. "And we were the first stop; they would be interrogated here and unless they could come up with something very plausible and had something in the way of identification, we sent them back to a bigger interrogation center."

This job went on until January 1945, when his team members started to be replaced, one by one, with interpreters who could speak German.

"The Army knew that it would eventually go into Germany," McKee said. "So I expected to be recalled, but then toward the end of January, early February we suddenly crashed across the German frontier, then crossed the Rhine. I kept sending messages back saying 'I know about two words of German and I'm no good' and never heard anything."

So, he drove a Jeep and sent reports, but had to stop interrogation work for a time.

"We followed sort of a peculiar course through Germany, going due east to begin with, and then turning south for Nuremberg, Dachau, Munich, and then east again toward Austria on the main road from Munich to Salzburg in Austria. On V-E day we were in Austria, in Salzburg."

McKee's team helped demobilize the German army in the Alps before going to Kornwestheim, a town near Stuttgart, where the U.S. Army had set up internment camps for German prisoners.

"Our camp, in the beginning, had about 10,000 prisoners," he said. "Our inmates were all suspected of having been concentration camp personnel, and they were pretty awful people, a lot of them. It was while I was there the Nuremberg trials were going on and some of these people committed suicide — it was sort of a messy thing. They got interrogated every day."

McKee took some German lessons from a citizen in the nearby town during this time, and bought some books to study the language.

"I was in the intelligence office at this prison camp and there were gigantic rosters of German names that went from the Americans to the British to the Russians to the French. And it kept circulating all the time if in the interrogations of prisoners you found out something about somebody else, you'd put that bit of information in, so you were building up information on all the names on the list. Some of those people, I'm sure, were taken off and executed."

At the end of September of '45 he had served his time in the Army. McKee returned to France on his way home, but was held up by a maritime strike — there were no boats back to the States.

"I went to Paris and the U.S. War Department headquarters was then established and had its offices in Paris, so I went to see them and said, 'Here is my situation.'" He got a government contract to work as an interpreter for the War Department until the following July. He took the opportunity to visit French people he had met both there and in the States beforehand.

"While I was there, they introduced me to a great many people who were in publishing houses, in newspapers, that kind of thing. So in the spring of '46 they said 'Why don't you stay? We can get you a work permit and we can get you a job.' So I thought to myself that would be more fun than going back to the job that had been kept for me at a prep school."

So McKee stayed in France until 1981, taking annual summer trips back to New York. He worked for a book publishing house and a literary agency, before he and a partner began their own agency in 1954.

Yet he was a teacher before the war, and he also taught two morning classes at the American School in Paris for 30 years. Now he keeps his hand in the classroom by visiting the Gilbertsville-Mount Upton High School about twice a month.

"I go over and speak with students in the French class," he said. "Some of them are very talented."

She says she is one of the lucky ones. And Monique Erlichman should know. She was a 12-year-old Jew living in France during World War II, when the Nazis ruled with an iron fist.

Literally marked as Jews, her family hid for more than two years, in constant danger of arrest. She, her sister and parents went undetected, while uncles and cousins disappeared — forever.

With the help of those who cared and by their own wits, they survived. That was 50 years ago.

"The Jews had to wear a Star of David, except anybody under (age) 15," she said, sitting in her Walton home. "Now, I know in other countries 5-, 6-, 7-year-old children had to wear it. My mother was a housewife; she refused to wear it. We'd get it on a piece of cloth, and then you'd have to cut it out and hem it and sew it onto the garment. No problem, because we had very few garments. It was usually on a coat.

"My father went to work and he wore it, but I remember he always took his newspaper and carried it like this to hide it," she said, holding a paper up over her heart. "It's a humiliating thing; you're marked like cattle. Plus the danger. One day my father came home from lunch before we went into hiding and there was a French police officer who stopped him coming out of the subway. And they'd ask you for your papers — and everybody who had Jewish papers was taken to trucks, and their families never saw them.

"And they came to my father. They had this stupid idea that the Jews are so rich and they own the world; my father was a factory worker," she said. "So the guy saw — I guess he had a heart — my father's occupation, and he said to him, 'Run! Get lost!' ... And if the man hadn't done that, we would have never seen my father again, and not known what happened to him. That's how you lived, from day to day."

In those days, her name was Monique Spiegel. Her father, Andre, was from Hungary and her mother, Frida, was Austrian. Though acts of anti-Semitism increased gradually, by July 1942 Jews in Paris were no longer safe.

"There was a woman who worked at the Hungarian consulate, where my father had been a national," she said. "She had been a friend of ours;

Never Safe

Holocaust survivor tells of years spent hiding from the Nazis

she lived in the same (apartment) house. And she went to our super and said, 'Tell the Spiegels to leave NOW. Tomorrow is the day.' Because apparently she came across a list of people who were to be arrested."

So the family moved overnight to a Parisian suburb called La Varenne-St. Hilaire, where they stayed almost a year, until April of '43. Her sister, Micheline, was almost 5 years old and Monique was nearly 13.

"It became very hard," she said. "In one incident we walked on the street and two little girls, young kids 8, 9 years old were pointing their finger at us and talking to each other said, 'Look, there's two Jews there.' They were trained to recognize — whether they were right or not. They could have pointed at an Italian who looked very Semitic and said the same thing.

"And the people who stuck their neck out were also slated. They were slated for destruction if they were discovered," she said. Her family stayed in the home of Susanne and Marcel Maloberti; Susanne worked with her father. They were employed by Lederer's, a fine leather manufacturer, and she was able to bring home work for him to do in the house.

"My father was a pocketbook maker and designer," she said. "Mr. Lederer was owner of several stores throughout the world; I think there's one in London, one in Rome or Milan, there was one in Paris and there was one in New York City which went out of business. They made magnificent things, very luxurious things. They worked mainly in crocodile.

"And during the war the biggest customers (business was very prosperous) were German officers because the mark was worth so much that to them the money was nothing, it was like water. So, little did they know when they bought these bags that they helped Jews survive. The man who managed the store was a German and all I have is his last name. The man provided work to all those people who were in hiding, and of course he knew. And not only that, but he paid them generously, which is another thing."

"My parents didn't go out of the house," Erlichman said. "So the lady who owned the house went out shopping and she delivered the merchandise. We weren't allowed to ride the train or the subway or the buses. In the subway, we were allocated the last car of the train. We couldn't use the restaurants, which was immaterial for us because we couldn't afford it anyway, we couldn't use a public telephone, we weren't allowed in post offices."

One night the front of the house was painted with the words "Jews hide here" and the Spiegels knew it was time to move their daughters to another location.

The owner of their clandestine home was a mason who worked in country towns.

"He found a lady nine kilometers away, outside of Normandy, in a little village called Montjavoult. ... The gentleman heard that this lady took boarders; it was a way of making a living. So he went there to that village and he stayed there, and every day he was taken by truck back to work.

"...So then he asked the lady, 'You live in the country here; it looks very nice and safe. Would you consider taking on two little Jewish girls and hiding them?' And she said, 'Of course. Bring them.' Just like that. And there was no money to be made, because we had no money. My mother gave me a little bit of something she stuck in a drawer, and (the lady) never touched it — because she sewed me a pocket inside my shorts so if we had an air raid or anything, I would take it with me."

This woman, Jeanne Lamboux, became an important person to the teen-age girl. Lamboux treated her more like an adult than her parents had. Erlichman and her sister began calling her "aunt."

There were many German troops around, but the girls never saw the feared SS or Gestapo. Two officers even stayed in the house.

"We had no choice; we were told what to do, we weren't asked," she said. "So, right next to my bedroom were two German officers.

"One of them had been on the Russian front, and he had a little girl about my sister's age, and he hadn't seen her in years. And he wanted to take her on his lap, and she went livid because she knew never go with a German — they are our enemies. And the man wanted just to give her a little affection."

An old woman in the village threatened to report them to authorities if she were sure they were Jews, because money was paid for such information. So, Erlichman started attending Catholic Mass.

To complete her disguise, Erlichman obtained false identity papers from the village mayor's assistant.

Monique Erlichman of Walton holds a cloth Star of David worn by her father during the Nazi occupation of France. All Jews aged 15 and over were required to wear the star, which says 'Jew' in French in its center. (Photo by Julie Lewis)

"He was also the head schoolmaster and he made false ID cards for everyone who was hiding there, from Jews to American parachutists to men who tried to escape obligatory work in Germany," she said. "For anyone who was hiding there, he made the thing and never, never charged a penny for it. The man was a communist. ...You met with an unbelievable amount of heroism, where people would not even think twice — that was the thing to do, that's all."

Paris was liberated from Nazi control in August 1944, so Erlichman's parents returned home. The liberation of Montjavoult in September by American forces is a memory vivid in Erlichman's mind.

"That day I got up and said, 'The Americans are here! The Americans are here!' jumped into my clothes, grabbed my little sister and the lady, and we went onto a back road. And the American tanks came by and we were jumping for joy and crying. There was no battle; all the Germans just came by with their arms up, surrounded."

Erlichman returned to school in Paris, reunited with her family. She moved to New York City in 1952, working first as a hairdresser and later as a respiratory therapist. She met her American husband, Norman, there and married at age 37.

They have had a summer home in the town of Walton for over 20 years, and moved there permanently in August 1992.

She has been back to France for visits over the years. Recently her interest in the past has been reawakened by a 1991 meeting with the International Congress of the Hidden Child, which held workshops for those forced to hide as youths during the war. Her desire is to try and locate descendants of those who saved her family's lives.

"My mother was the soul and the heart and the strength, the pillar of the family," she said. "A little bit of a woman, shorter than I am. She had a hard life too, but was very strong."

Brothers In Arms

John and Charlie Gallagher remember D-Day 50 years later

John and Charlie Gallagher of Oneonta were part of what General Dwight D. Eisenhower called "the Great Crusade" during World War II.

Operation Overlord, the invasion of northern France, was the Allies' complex strategy to wrestle the European continent from the grasp of Nazism, freeing hundreds of millions of people.

Though John was sergeant of a platoon that landed on D-Day 50 years ago today on Utah beach, his younger brother, Charlie, was a radioman in the army's 3rd Armored Division that arrived five days later.

They hadn't seen each other in three years. After fighting with their companies day after day, the brothers had a surprise in early July.

"We had trouble with one of our outposts, and when I was going over to the outpost I saw the code name for my brother's outfit," John said. "But I wasn't about to walk in there at night. We were preparing for the St. Lo breakthrough.

"So the next day, as luck would have it, we didn't do much so I went over and saw my brother. The headquarters was right up front at the field, and I asked if there was a Gallagher in that outfit, and he said, 'Yes, he's right down there.' So I went down in and asked, 'Charlie Gallagher?' and then I said 'B' (his nickname) and he knew who I was."

"I didn't recognize him with his beard," Charlie said. "You see, he had a nice goatee."

It turned out their divisions were working together to gain the town of St. Lo, about 25 miles inland.

Charlie was in a mortar squad with the job of stringing wire for the field telephones.

"You had to string wire and hook them up and hope they work," he said. "And about the time you strung a couple of hundred yards across from one hedgerow to the next, a shell would hit it and there wouldn't be any wire... it would be gone."

They compared notes that day, and the next day Charlie was able to visit John's outfit before they were separated again.

On D-Day John was fired on by small arms and artillery — including the mortars Allies dubbed Screaming Meemies, for their high-pitched noise.

John Gallagher (left) stands in a slit trench by his brother, Charlie, sitting on his helmet in Normandy before the St. Lo breakthrough in 1944.

Oneonta brothers Charlie (left) and John Gallagher with a map of the Normandy invasion and the helmet John wore on D-Day. (Photo by Julie Lewis)

"They'd scream and at least a dozen would be fired at once," he said. "If you were a veteran you could tell about where they'd land, so you didn't bother to jump in a hole, but those who didn't know would run for cover. And then they got smart and they put oil on them, so when they hit they'd set the men on fire."

Anyone in combat had a tough time, but some jobs are always worse than others, he said.

"When tanks got hit, they didn't have a chance. The paratroopers and the glider troops had a terrible time; when the gliders came down, they'd hit a tree or some of the posts that the Germans had put up, or a house and they were dead. The Germans put these posts maybe six feet high in a field so these glider troops couldn't come in — if they hit the posts, they would rip them all apart.

"And at night, those posts would look like men and they'd scare the hell out of you. A guy would run a bayonet into a post."

Between the time that the brothers met and St. Lo was taken, Charlie read in Stars and Stripes, a newspaper for servicemen, that John had received a battlefield commission and a Silver Star. John became a lieutenant, while Charlie remained a private first class.

"When I saw him the first time I didn't have to salute him. A few days later, I had to," Charlie said with a grin. "Not really."

Between the beach and Ste.-Mere-Eglise the Germans had flooded fields in an effort to stop invading troops.

"They had big ditches, 6, 7 feet deep, and if you stepped in that with a pack on and a helmet, you tipped over and drowned," John said. "There was nothing you could do; you can't help them. They were gone, that's all."

Later, forging their way to St. Lo went much slower than expected.

"His company was to push a hole in the road, breach the road, and we were to take a hill 25 miles away — in one day," Charlie said. "In one day. You know how far we went? We went 100 yards the first day."

John served with the 4th Infantry Division and was wounded by a mine the day before troops freed Paris in August 1944. Yet, being wounded didn't compare to the thousands that were lost in the invasion.

"I finally figured, there were 26 of us left who had landed on D-Day out of 180 in our company, by the time we took Cherbourg (at the end of June)," John said. "You know, a lot of men were killed on D-Day who never even got on shore, because the ramp went down too soon and they drowned or they were killed by obstacles that were mined."

The Gallaghers were awarded European Theater of Operations Battle Stars and Combat Infantry Badges. John also received a Purple Heart. Charlie earned a Bronze Star with an Oakleaf Cluster. Yet strangely enough, over the years the brothers never talked much about their roles in the invasion.

"You see so many friends that you had lived with for three years get killed," John said. "You know, you're kind of punch-drunk after a while. You can look at my eyes in that picture and tell that I've had it."

Charlie agreed. "I've never really thought too much about it," he said. "You're just damn lucky, and glad you got through it."

On the beach, in the line of fire, Marino Scorzafava destroyed barriers

Marino Scorzafava picked up another bundle of dynamite and tied it to the steel and concrete barrier blocking Omaha Beach. German guns and mortars raked the sand. Offshore, the big guns of the U.S. Navy pounded the German positions on the cliffs.

Thousands of troops were already wading through the surf and thousands more were in landing craft heading toward the shore.

If they were going to get off the beach, they would need a way through. At 6:30 a.m. on June 6, 1944, Scorzafava and his fellow frogmen slogged from barrier to barrier, blowing 50-yard gaps in the line and opening the door to France.

Amphibious tanks sank in the surf and rubber boats full of TNT exploded. Only Scorzafava and one other frogman from his crew survived.

At times, they found themselves fighting like combat soldiers instead of the Naval frogmen they were trained to be.

"We picked up rifles off dead soldiers and were hiding behind dead soldiers. And the wounded were screaming and hollering for medics and corpsmen."

For more than four decades he kept his thoughts about those days to himself. Only his sister, Faustina Russo, knew that he was in a secret demolition unit. And only after she died and the family was sorting through some papers did his wife, Jean, and son, Charles, find out about his role. Only then did they understand how he lost part of his hearing and why he sometimes had nightmares.

Even now, he has trouble coping with what happened.

"I could talk to you for a whole week, and I could never tell you the whole, true story. We were crucified; a terrible, terrible, terrible situation."

The Longest Day June 6, 1944

Marino Scorzafava in late 1944.

Scorzafava was later awarded the Victory Medal, the French Croix de Guerre, two stars from the European Theater, a Bronze Star, two Purple Hearts and a Presidential Unit Citation from Harry S. Truman. After the war, he returned to Oneonta and worked for the D&H Railroad. He was married in 1949 and later served as an alderman.

On D-Day, Scorzafava landed with the first wave of troops under heavy German artillery, machine-gun and sniper fire. The Naval Combat Demolition Unit worked alongside Army demolition crews to blow up the obstacles which were exposed then, at low tide, but would be covered as the tide came in.

Landing craft and tanks sent to support the 16 demolition units were hit and set on fire. Nearly half the amphibious tanks approaching land foundered and sank in the heaving swells.

The 13-man unit had a rubber supply boat full of dynamite, TNT and plastic explosives. The men carried one- and two-pound charges in packs tied around their chests. As they worked their way down the beach, they would tie the charges to the barriers.

"We had to tie each charge individually; we'd tie a whole 50-yard gap and blow it with primer cord that attached one explosive to the other," he said. Grabbing more charges where they could, his group moved across the beach, clearing safe channels for the landing craft to touch down.

After exhausting the explosives in their chest packs, Scorzafava and his crew members were to restock from the supply in a rubber boat nearby.

"But that got hit and killed the guy that was holding it, to start with. That was gone. And then all havoc broke loose and they were dying like flies," he said slowly.

"The group this side of us got killed, and two groups over, they got killed — everybody," he said recently, pointing to a map he drew at his Oneonta home. "A big 88 shell hit the small boat, landing craft, and blew them out; we couldn't find them."

The path to the beach turned fatal for some men coming out of the landing craft.

"Every one of these things was mined, with several different kinds of mines. If you touched one of those, it blew you to bits," he said.

"The obstacles were roughly 4 1/2, 5 feet high. And the soldiers were hiding behind them for protection, because they were getting shot up by snipers. So I went out to one guy and I told him, 'You get out of the way — we've got to blow these.'

"And I got him and pulled him away, and right away he was back in there because he was partly drowning and he was probably frightened like the rest of us, and he froze," he said, his voice soft with compassion. "And I pulled him off and then I couldn't do any more. So we killed

Marino Scorzafava of Oneonta holds a citation for the Victory Medal from President Truman for his World War II service. (Photo by Julie Lewis)

some of our own, blew some of our own up, we had to." He threw his arm out as if gesturing out toward sea.

"Because you've got thousands upon thousands of soldiers behind you coming in that day," he said. "And this was the immediate hour. That's the thing that bothered me the most, we blew our own boys up. Guys our own age at the time, we were only early 20s, 19, 18."

Help finally arrived on D-Day, with reinforcements from Utah Beach.

"They didn't have quite the opposition; they had opposition, but no comparison," he said.

"We were supposed to be on that beach, us, maybe a couple hours. I was on there three weeks, cleaning up the devastation, the mess and the dead."

Marshall Smith in 1946.

Sweeping mines, and survivors Marshall Smith helped to keep the channel to Normandy open

On D-Day and for the next few weeks, Marshall Smith kept his eyes on the waters of the English Channel looking for two things: survivors to pick up and mines to explode.

He was 18 then, part of a crew he calls "the rawest of rookies you ever saw in your life," most with less than three years of service in the Navy, out on their first sea duty.

Smith, who lives in Otego, was aboard a wooden minesweeper, the YMS 349, which held 36 men and four officers on its 136 feet.

There were six yard minesweepers in his flotilla, and they spent the first half of 1944 performing exercises and a mock invasion in the Irish Sea. Although the sailors couldn't discuss

military plans on shore, among themselves the thought was they were in England to invade the French coast.

"But of course, nobody ever knew," he said. "It was the greatest kept secret the world has ever known.

"And then the last week of May, no more liberty, no more leave, couldn't leave the ship for nothing," he said.

On the night of June 3, Smith's flotilla left Plymouth harbor to rendezvous near Southampton with other ships. But the weather suddenly turned bad and the ships were sent back.

At dusk on June 5, they got the word to start again and took the same route, then headed across the English Channel. The minesweepers went ahead of the larger ships to pick up mines magnetically and explode them, before they could do their deadly damage.

"The first week was hell; D-Day was bad. We were picking up survivors, we were sweeping channels in and marking buoys, so our ships could go in," he said. There were acoustic mines that were blown up through sound emitted by a hammer.

"Then you had magnetic tails that went off maybe 200 yards off the stern of your ship," he said. "They had electrical charges and they would cause a magnetic field that would draw the mines, then you'd blow them. Then there were the moored mines that most people see, with the things on them that come to the top, and we cut the cables on them and we had automatic charges that would blow those mines up."

All day they blew up mines and picked up survivors, who were kept on board until a hospital ship could take them. Smith's flotilla was primarily off of Omaha Beach.

"It got scary, it got scary a lot of times when we were going in and sweeping as close as we could get, and dropping these buoys over to mark channels," he said. "With two minesweepers abreast we could probably make a swath in there and put buoys down marking channels 200 yards that we'd swept. We'd have different lanes; we were trying to cover 30 miles of beaches and make lanes in where landing craft could go in.

"But we were interrupted picking up survivors all the time. We'd see them floating by, and of course if there was no life there, we'd just let them keep on going," Smith said slowly. "And that was something new to a person like myself because you'd be up telling the petty officer on the deck, 'There are GIs floating by, there are sailors floating by.' ... And we just weren't allowed to pick them up. We couldn't do anything with the dead. If they had life, we'd pick them up."

Although the minesweepers were first in line, they weren't targeted by the Germans at first.

"You could tell whether you were a target ship or not, the way the shells were coming," Smith said. "Invariably they were after the landing craft, amphibious ships, the LSTs, the LCIs and all of that. They knew what was coming ashore. So they didn't bother us that much."

Although mines posed a constant danger, what really got to Smith and his fellow mates was the bloodbath taking place on shore.

"...It was terrible, and you're looking through the binoculars, and you're looking at guys getting blown apart," he said. "You see direct hits on the landing craft, and it doesn't get to you at first. ... You see guys swimming onshore, and you see everything that's going on on the beach.

"You get these destroyers, every once in a while you'd have to imagine they got a call and all of a sudden they're runnin' in and their guns are just blowing the beaches apart. We were prob-

Marshall Smith's ship, the Y.M.S. 349 is in the background as soldiers board landing craft on June 3, 1944, in England. This photo appeared in the Stars and Stripes, a newspaper for U.S. servicemen.

Marshall Smith of Otego stands in front of American Legion Post 259 in Oneonta. (Photo by Julie Lewis)

CAROOM," Smith said, and paused. "She hit a mine. She was gone in 10 minutes' time. We picked up survivors; anybody who was below deck, they were gone. I think our ship picked up five. With the other sweepers who got there first, I think we picked up about 12, out of 36 and four officers.

"We had been sweeping this area for almost two weeks. We were catching hell, a lot of times, that we'd lay our buoys that the channels were clear of mines. Three and four weeks later, ships were coming in and they were getting hit by mines. What we had heard, and we never knew this, because I was a gunners mate and of course I went to minesweeper's school, was that they had counter mines.

"And what a counter mine was, it lay on the bottom. And the Germans would set it till a ship would go over it so many times; the time it was set for, it would come and blow 'em," he said. "We never heard of it; that was one of their great surprises."

Smith's duty took him to the south of France and later to Hawaii and Saipan, preparing to invade Japan. And in spite of all the stress of war, he loved being on a ship. He thought of re-enlisting when the war was over, but decided to get married instead. He and his second wife, Audrey, have six sons and one daughter.

Since his retirement six years ago, Smith has thought about the war more than during the 40 years afterward. This month he comes full circle in a way, when he becomes commander of the Oneonta American Legion Friday.

To him, the military has a personal value as well as a national one.

"You're never as close again when you're an adult as you are when you're in grade school and high school when you have close friends," Smith said. "And you go in the service, and it magnifies into a bigger thing.

"You learn that you depend on the guys on your right and the guys on your left. You get to depend on everybody that's concerned with you. And that's the only place that you ever learn that."

ably having a hard time with our troops," he said. "You see it all your waking hours, you're on watch. It just gets to you."

The minesweepers anchored about six miles off the beach, and kept up their daily sweeping of mines, which went from dawn to dark. Averaging no more than five hours of sleep a day, one day started to run into the next.

The Germans could keep placing mines because the Allies still hadn't captured Norway — and submarines came from ports there. And no matter how many passes the minesweepers made, danger was ever-present.

"We were making one last run this late afternoon, and the YMS 350 wanted to make one more run in close to the seawall on the outside and that would be her last run. We were heading back, and we got about 400 yards and we heard a

Paratrooper saw war from above – William Hughes wounded in air

William Hughes jumped out of his C-47 shortly after midnight on June 6, 1944, and had already been wounded in the air.

He was hit in both legs, but he was jump master — the first paratrooper to jump after the plane cleared the searchlights. When he landed in Normandy, about 15 miles inland from Omaha Beach, he gathered 12 squad members together in the dark to set off on their mission.

He was a member of the parachute infantry with the 101st Airborne Division. His plane was part of an "air train" 250 miles long, with fighters, bombers and airborne divisions carrying 18,000 men to launch the assault on Nazi-occupied France.

It was his squad's first time in combat and anti-aircraft fire found them as they flew over France.

"Everybody went their different ways and so we were just helter-skelter all over the place," the Oneonta man said. "Nobody knew exactly where they were."

Trying to avoid the fire, the plane was caught in a town's searchlights.

"Our pilot was killed, I found out later, and the crew chief was killed," he said. "Our evasive action was to fly right down the main street of that town. We were about 200, 300 feet high and searchlights were on us and they were pumping anti-aircraft into us like mad."

The squad lost one member in the jump, but there were no other fatalities until later battles, when many of them were killed.

"Out of that squad of mine, I'm the only one alive today," he said. "There was one survivor that I know of; a fellow in Pennsylvania. He and I were

William Hughes of Oneonta holds a photo of himself that was taken at age 19 in 1942. (Photo by Julie Lewis)

the only two that survived out of that squad. The rest of them were all killed in action, in Holland or in Bastogne. He just died a few years ago. So, I don't have any desire to go back there — none whatsoever."

Fifty years ago, Hughes had to lead the other paratroopers through the fields toward the beach. His legs stopped bleeding after a while, and he wrapped them with sulfa drugs and bandages as he and his group struggled to get organized and move toward the beach. In the confusion, they used metal "crickets" that clicked in the dark, to signal with friendly troops.

"Basically we tried to stay in the fields, because we didn't know what was on the roads; any tanks or weapons," he said. "At night we didn't have any idea, but in daylight we could see where we were heading: it was easy to take your compass readings and see the map. So we'd fight all day and try to hole up at night."

In the disorganization of men trying to find their outfits, his group grew to about 25 men as it traveled; two of his squad were separated during the jump and met up with them days later. Moving toward Omaha, they encountered pockets of Germans and took about 15 prisoners before getting close to the beach three days later. He spoke a little German and could make himself understood.

"It was exciting," Hughes said. "We were nervous, scared. But we were well-trained. We knew exactly what we had to do and we did it. ... You're never prepared, really, to see people shot or killed, but it happens.

"When I got to an aid station, the doctor there looked at me and said 'You're going back to England.' I was all done fighting there."

After being taken to the beach by truck, Hughes was put aboard a ship to Great Britain. He spent 10 days in the hospital and at age 22 lost one leg from his wounds. When his company returned to England Hughes rejoined it, later fighting in the invasion of Holland and the Battle of the Bulge, in Bastogne. He made a total of more than 30 jumps.

Born in Scotland but raised in Oneonta, after the war he and his wife, Peggy, were married and had five children. He retired from Bendix Corp. in Sidney in 1983.

Henry Schebaum saw joy, horror on the sea

Henry Schebaum's job on D-Day was to keep his "tin can" moving. He worked in the engine room of the U.S.S. *Barton*, a newly commissioned Navy destroyer that held about 300 men.

"It was very cloudy and overcast," the Morris man said. "I stood my watches in the engine room, but I do remember standing on deck and just looking around, and all you could see was ships, everywhere – all over.

"One of the most vivid things I remember was seeing the bodies of soldiers floating around on the water. There weren't a lot of them, because we were about a mile off-shore... But then there was a happy event. A lot of the equipment that they were sending ashore with the troops was on flat barges, they were nothing but just a plain float, maybe 20 by 25-feet square with a big outboard engine on them," he said.

"One of these had capsized and we managed to pick up all the soldiers who were on it; there were only eight or 10, something like that. You can understand, they were very happy soldiers. And they stayed with us for a good part of the time we were off the coast of France."

Destroyers off Normandy were on the lookout for U-boats, German Unterseeboote, or "undersea boats" that were armed with torpedoes and could sometimes stay submerged for 18 hours. Destroyers like the Barton were also prepared to give anti-aircraft support with their 5-inch guns.

"In connection with the invasion, we formed up a group, I think with one of the old battleships, the Texas or the Mississippi, one of the real old ones, a couple of cruisers, and four destroyers – four in a division," Schebaum said. "And they sent us down to the harbor of Cherbourg to break down the shore defenses and see if they could open up the port of Cherbourg, so they could bring in the supplies and more men into France, instead of all going across the beach in Normandy.

"This is the closest I came to any danger. I was asleep; I was off watch. And the other com-

Henry Schebaum of Morris stands with a Navy advertisement from a magazine during the war years. (Photo by Julie Lewis)

partment where I was sleeping was hit by an 8-inch shell. Fortunately the shell didn't explode, or I wouldn't be here," he said.

"The chief metalsmith on the ship, and I don't remember his name now, he went in there and he picked that shell up and he threw it back out the hole it made coming in. Can you imagine that? He got a decoration and he deserved every bit of that."

Being below deck in the engine room, it was hard for machinist's mates like Schebaum to know what was happening outside. "We had a chief engineer who would stay up on the main deck right by the engine room hatch," he said. "And he had a phone set on, and he could give us a running account of what was going on, so we would have some idea."

The Barton was off the French coast for three or four weeks, then sent back to England. Before that, Schebaum spent three years on the U.S.S. *Greer*, which acted as an escort on the North Atlantic.

He had thought about staying in the Navy. But he was offered a job with Long Island Lighting Company, doing the same job he'd done on the ship: running boilers and steam turbines.

He and his wife, Mary, married after the war. She had been a sergeant in the WACs, and they later had two children, William and Lauren. They moved upstate 10 years ago.

"I learned my trade in the Navy and made my living with it the rest of the time, 38 years," he said.

They were all over town before the war: in school, playing baseball, walking down the street. Many came from Oneonta, but also from Milford, Portlandville and other towns across the state. They were the boys of Company G.

Part of the New York State National Guard, in October 1940 Company G was mustered into federal service in October 1940, more than a year before the U.S. entered World War II. Former schoolmates trained side by side in Alabama before shipping out for Hawaii after the Japanese attacked Pearl Harbor.

Yet Oneonta's August Gardella had been a member of Company G from 1934-37, and had taken work on Long Island in 1939. Drafted in early 1941, he was assigned to the 105th Infantry, but as wartime neared he got a transfer back to the 106th in Company G. He was back with his friends by the fall of '41.

After landing in Hawaii to protect the islands in 1942, Gardella ended up feeding the troops as a first cook in field kitchens set up beneath tents.

But that changed when the company went into combat. After a month on Majuro in the Marshall Islands, American forces headed for Japanese strongholds in the Marianas: Saipan, Tinian and Guam. The islands were important for two reasons — if captured, American planes would be within bombing distance of mainland Japan; and they lay across the Allied invasion route to the Japanese-held Philippines.

For these reasons the battles would be decisive. On June 11, 1944, aircraft from four naval carrier groups bombed airfields on Saipan, Tinian and Guam. U.S. battleships shelled Saipan on June 13 and 14, and at dawn on June 15 before the first assault troops landed.

Yet there were 32,000 Japanese ready to defend Saipan. In spite of Allied pounding from the air and sea, many camouflaged strongholds went unscathed on the 25-mile-long island.

After the Marines invaded, more help was sent ashore in the form of the Army's 27th Infantry Division. After several days, Gardella and other Company G soldiers handled supplies and took them to the front. He was later integrated with the company and took part in a mopping up operation.

The Men Of Company G

Fifty years ago, Oneonta area infantryman fought across the Pacific

August Gardella, a former member of Company G, holds a guidon from 1940 at the New York State Armory gymnasium in Oneonta. He trained and stayed at the armory briefly before combat in World War II. (Photo by Julie Lewis)

After 22 days of fierce combat, on July 7 about 3,000 Japanese staged a *banzai* charge on his division. With suicidal determination they broke through American lines, some with only rifles and bayonets.

"They just came charging and were mowed down by our men," said Gardella, 81. "They didn't care about life. And there was a cliff on the island there, that a lot of them jumped over and committed suicide — not many soldiers, but some of the Japanese civilians. I guess they were told that we would torture them."

Nearly 3,500 Americans died on Saipan and more than 13,000 were wounded. Afterward, some members of Company G and other infantry went on to invade Okinawa in April 1945. Yet, the men who were lost were far from forgotten.

In 1946 Oneonta City Historian R.A. Johnson compiled a booklet entitled "Our Gold Star Men" that includes war records and photos of 60 Oneonta area men who gave their lives during World War II. The names of 2,000 other men and women who served from this community are also listed. The end of its dedication reads:

> *To those men who died as becomes Americans, whose love of country filled their hearts; And to their survivors who must have an unfaltering resolution to build a good world for all, and to keep the peace for which they so nobly died.*

Those who
didn't return

Both a plaque hanging in the New York State Armory on Academy Street in Oneonta and the booklet "Our Gold Star Men" compiled by R.A. Johnson, former Oneonta city historian, pay tribute to the men of G Company who were killed during World War II. Named are:

James W. Imhoff, Nicholas C. Rosher Jr., Louis S. Super, Henry E. Markle, Ernest S. Price, Lester C. Borst, John F. Brienza, Charles Spoor, Ralph T. Marino, Frederick R. Heck, Lloyd Mayo, David "Bill" Hodges, and Henry Spargo.

Out Of Adversity

Area veterans were in the medical corps during WWII

Emma Porteus

When the inevitable happened in World War II and American soldiers were wounded on a foreign battlefield, members of the next front stepped forward: those serving in the medical corps. Alberta A. Bowes of Cooperstown volunteered.

"I was assigned to the 25th Hospital Train Unit," she said. "It was a unit unto itself." Medical staff lived on the 18-car train, which carried 320 patients when fully loaded, she said.

"Our trips might last anywhere from two or three days to over three weeks at a time, before we got back to Paris," where orders originated, Bowes said. Raised in Oneonta, she had graduated from nursing school in the spring of 1943 and landed in France in January of '45 with the Army Nurse Corps.

One car carried 60 ambulatory patients — those who could sit up or move. Eight "litter cars" held three tiers of litters, or stretchers, in each. Two doctors were on board, one who was train commander, along with four nurses and a pharmacist.

"We were essentially an evacuation and triage (evaluation) unit; we picked patients up from various places. We were often at the front," she said.

Working six hours on and six hours off, the train's four nurses worked two at a time, dividing the cars of wounded between them. More seriously wounded soldiers were placed on the lower litters for frequent treatment.

Trains traveled with a large red cross on the top of each car for visibility to the enemy, to encourage hospital neutrality. Hospital trains had priority on the tracks second only to munitions trains, Bowes said. Yet their safety was far from ensured.

While loading wounded onto the train in Belgium, an ambulance was hit by a V-2 bomb and everyone inside it killed. Another time, the train was hit by tracer bullets, which started a fire in the storage area. Yet the fear of being killed by bombs and the horror of the pain and death surrounding her had to take second place to the vast amount of work to be done, Bowes said.

"You could hear the V-2 bombs, unmanned rocket types of things.... But you didn't think much about this. Everybody was experiencing it, so that's the way it was," she said.

The 170th General Hospital where Emma Porteus served southeast of Paris in 1944.

"I think we were rather upbeat, because we felt we were helping people from our country. I had a brother in the Navy and some of the others had family in the service, so you felt in a way you were helping them, too."

Also on the move, behind the fighting troops, were the field hospitals. Ed McMahon of Westville joined the Army medical corps in 1942. After training at a dental school in Springfield, Mo., he was assigned to the 1st Army's 47th Field Hospital, landing in Normandy several weeks after D-Day.

"We were always slotted as close as practical to where the fighting was going on," McMahon said. "Now, I don't mean we're a mile behind the lines. Probably the closest we got was four to six miles back, because there's no point in pulling up where you can't operate. There are smaller medical stations right there on the line.

"What they were able to accomplish with field hospitals in general, was that within maybe an hour's time of some poor kid getting hit, he'd be on the operating table — a lot of times it would be within 20 minutes."

Field hospitals traditionally only took chest and stomach wounds, McMahon said, noting that those were the killers. Often the hospital was set up in tents about 25 by 35 feet, linked together in the form of a cross, with about 200 people working: doctors, nurses and enlisted men. The tents were arranged to operate as three separate units, or to combine as a single larger one.

"Ambulances would back up to the tent, they'd bring in these people and they'd probably have sawhorses and they'd just set the litters between two sawhorses. ...Incidentally, there'd always be a tag about this long tied on him," he said, holding his hands eight or nine inches apart. This "field jacket" was a short medical history on which each person treating the patient recorded shots and medication given.

After determining patient priority, operations took place, then soldiers were sent to the "shock ward" or recovery area. Later they were moved to the regular ward tent, lying on canvas cots and thin mattresses, with sheets and blankets.

"We would keep such a patient for perhaps two weeks. If we could keep him alive and see the progress being made, we had done our job,"

Emma Porteus (seated), Ed McMahon, and Alberta A. Bowes hold the flag of the American Red Cross, used during the war to identify medical tents. On the table are a Bible issued by the government during the war, an army patch from the Nurse Army Corps and the American Red Cross, and a blood pressure kit. (Photo by Julie Lewis)

McMahon said. "He would then be evacuated further back to a larger hospital."

To identify hospitals, each tent had a huge white circle on the side, in addition to four large canvases painted white with a red cross on top, secured to the ground nearby.

"I do recall in Holland, regularly a German plane would come over, usually late afternoon, firing — strafing — and stop as he was approaching the hospital," McMahon said. "He would zoom over so low you could really see the guy up in the canopy of the plane. ...They were after legitimate targets."

In addition to doing some dental work on soldiers, McMahon worked in the hospital lab. In September of 1944, the pharmacist he worked with was transferred and McMahon was asked to take an inventory of supplies. Suddenly they were ordered to Holland.

"I presume that they requisitioned a general pharmacist, but meanwhile I was there," he said. "They sent me back for a week with an evacuation hospital pharmacist and I spent intensive, around-the-clock work with him. And I worked with one of our own pharmacists, from one of the other hospital units of the 47th."

So, McMahon became a pharmacist making iodine, cough medicine and prescriptions for bronchitis from scratch. Other medications came prepared.

During the following winter, he was at a station hospital in Spa, Belgium, which was headquarters of the 1st Army. As a station hospital, the staff treated less wounded soldiers, but more with illnesses.

"You had all these guys and they're out there in the snow and the sleet and the rain, including all this big group of the 1st Army headquarters who had everything from appendicitis to broken legs to car accidents to pneumonia," he said.

Emma Porteus of Oneonta also treated a wide range of ailments during the war. Joining the Army Nurse Corps through the American Red Cross, she was sent to France to the 170th General Hospital, being established 120 miles southeast of Paris in July of '44.

They cared not only for Allied soldiers, but civilians caught in the crossfire and injured German prisoners of war. Located near Le Mans, the hospital operated like a city, with medical tents in the center, surrounded by quarters for nurses and soldiers.

"The first six months, I was in charge of five wards with 20, 24 people in each ward and I had one corpsman on a ward," Porteus said. Corpsmen served as assistants in the wards.

Previously trained as a nurse anesthetist, Porteus was transferred to the operating room, applying general anesthesia under a doctor's supervision.

"If a female in the Army came in for an operation, instead of giving anesthesia, I assisted in the operation instead of having a corpsman," she said. "It was quite unique; so I had experience in the whole works."

She and other nurses worked and lived in fatigues, four to a tent. Living wasn't easy or comfortable: They washed their hair using helmets as sinks, and in the winter had to find wood from the countryside to fuel their tent wood stoves. The late Cecelia Manion, an Oneonta native who worked at Fox Hospital, also served with Porteus in France.

Porteus described the constant activity and stress of the medical work as similar to the old "M*A*S*H*" television program.

"You were in so much activity, you just didn't learn to relax for a while," she said.

Porteus also said that the pain of the wounded and dying was hard to take at times. Often they cried and turned away after a soldier's death.

"It's very frustrating, especially when you see the younger ones," she said. "But it was wonderful to see the ones that were hurt and could go back to their units. The seriously ill were sent home."

Both Porteus and Bowes continued nursing careers after the war, Porteus in the operating room at Wilson Memorial Hospital in Johnson City, and Bowes teaching at Hartwick College before becoming director of nursing at Bassett Hospital in Cooperstown.

In spite of all the bloodshed and thousands who died, Porteus said there were some medical lessons gleaned from World War II.

"We used to keep the patients in bed for so long. If you had a hernia operation, they'd keep you in bed a week," she said. "But we had to get people up because we had so many more coming in. You recuperated so much better, the quicker you became active... Out of adversity, you learn new things."

Bowes saw Dachau camp

Alberta A. Bowes had an opportunity at the end of the war in Europe that most people have only read about: to visit the concentration camp at Dachau, Germany, days after its prisoners were freed.

"It was towards the end of April, the first part of May we were down in Munich, having just taken patients down to that area," said the Cooperstown woman who served as an army nurse during World War II. "And the concentration camp, Dachau, had been liberated about a week before that. We received information that if any of us were interested in going to see that we could do so, that they would have a truck to take us."

Most of the prisoners had been evacuated, but some who had arrived later and were not too ill were at the camp acting as guides for visitors.

"They took you through the barracks, and of course they hadn't really been cleaned up. One of the things you noticed as you approached, even before you got to the camp, was the stench. The smell was terrible. Different diseases have different odors and these were all mingled, along with the odor that comes with death and putrefaction."

Since the barracks hadn't been cleaned, the group saw the camp's living conditions as they had been, Bowes said.

"There were still parts of human skeletons in the creamatorium, which we saw. And we saw the gas chambers," she said slowly. "There were still things that they had removed from the corpses after they had killed them, or burned them. Dentures: they would take those out and remove the gold or silver from them and these were still piled on tables."

Bowes had small preparation for what she saw, although her hospital train had carried some Slavic and Polish prisoners from Nazi slave labor camps. Many had been critically ill, with diseases such as tuberculosis.

"The so-called 'strawberry beds' where they had planks laid over the ground and if for whatever reason they shot any of the inmates, which I guess they did fairly often, they would just leave the bodies on these and let them drain of blood before they threw them into the pits. All these things were still there," she said softly.

"So, it was an eye-opener I think, to all of us, and you really realized that it was necessary to have gone to war to prevent this from spreading throughout the world."

Because of this experience, in July of last year Bowes was interviewed for a documentation of the Holocaust, called "Witness to History." She was filmed in Albany with about 30 other people, all telling of their contact with concentration camps. The film is now at the Holocaust Memorial Museum in Washington, D.C.

"It upsets me a bit when I hear people saying these things never happened, because there were terrible things that did happen," she said.

Byron Sheesley had his B-17 at 23,000 feet when he looked out the cockpit window and saw the plane's left engine in flames.

"There were two fire extinguishers on each engine, and I hit the button for the fire extinguisher and the fire went out," he said. "And then very shortly, it started to burn again."

So, Sheesley knew he had to dive.

A member of the 8th Air Force in the 34th Bomb Group, Sheesley flew 35 missions over Germany starting 50 years ago this month. He and his crew were still over France and hadn't reached their factory and airfield targets when they lost their engine.

"My engineer thought it got hit with flak, but I think what really happened was that one of the cylinders blew and we lost all the oil," he said. "Normally, if you see something wrong with an engine you can push a button and it'll 'feather' the propellers so that it heads into the wind directly.

"But if you can't feather it, it flattens out so that it goes at its fastest speed. And without any oil in the cylinders, it got very, very hot and caught fire."

After leveling off at 3,000 feet, Sheesley told the crew to drop the bombs, which hadn't yet been armed, or set to go off.

"I knew we couldn't fly and carry that load, so we just dropped them and they probably wouldn't explode at all."

At that point he decided to turn back, but found he had another problem.

"When we got down to that level, my navigator became confused because his gyrocompass spilled on the way down so it was reading the wrong direction for him. And he didn't realize this had happened," he said.

"But I had a compass right in front of me and I knew my direction, and we could see the Alps in southern France. But I knew where I had to go, and I knew I didn't want to fly into the Alps — we could never get over them, anyway."

Heading west to return, the engine caught fire again. Hitting the button for the second extinguisher, Sheesley was surprised when it put the fire out. But the engine had a heavy vibration, from

Against A Wall Of Wind

Laurens man recalls adventure in skies over France during WW II

Byron Sheesley

After landing in England, Lt. Byron Sheesley surveys where the engine was lost from his B-17.

The extreme movement made them an easy target for the Germans, who began shooting at the aircraft as it passed over an occupied town in southern France.

"It was very hard to control the plane," Sheesley said. "The gunners down on the ground had our direction and our altitude perfectly and we could see these shells exploding right towards us, right direct on the nose. So I pushed real hard on the right rudder, and the plane just slid sideways and the bombs went right by us."

The engine was held on the wing by three bolts, one on top and two on the sides. And as the gunners below stopped shooting, the top bolt broke and the engine slowly peeled down and fell off.

"Then the wing was more stable, it didn't flap so much, but still we had this huge, flat surface where the engine was attached — we were flying against a wall of wind," he said. "And we still couldn't fly very fast. So we had to fly with the left wing up, sort of sideways, like this."

As the Flying Fortress kept losing airspeed, Sheesley told the crew to throw everything possible from the plane, to lighten it. The only thing that makes him laugh now is the memory of his navigator.

its speeding shaft without any oil, and the plane was unbalanced as they flew.

"The wing was flapping up and down — the end of it was going up about 10 feet, up and down like this, like a bird's wing," he said, moving his arm to the side. "We were afraid the whole wing would fall off."

"I knew I was heading in the right direction and my navigator kept telling me to turn around, because he was looking at a broken compass."

The radio operator reached three finding stations that gave them a heading, or direction, back to England, which was close to the way they'd been going. Sheesley dropped the plane down to 2,000 feet where the air was thicker and gave them more lift, as they headed across the English Channel. Aside from the danger of an unsafe plane, they were suddenly in a different predicament.

"The heading that they gave us — we couldn't believe it — but they took us right directly over the center of London and we were sure that they would shoot us down. Because nobody was supposed to fly over London," he said shaking his head.

The return flight took about four hours, and after escaping the final barrage of flak, Sheesley thought they might make it to their field in Mendelsham if he could keep the plane in the air.

"As much as I was able to control it and keep it flying, I knew that I could give my crew time to escape and I thought that I'd have time to jump out, too, if it looked like it wasn't going to make it," he said.

Because Sheesley did survive, he affected the lives of many area people. After graduating from medical school in 1952, he and his wife, Mary, moved to Stamford in 1958, where he set up a practice. In 1965 he moved to Oneonta and joined Dr. Virgil Polley in a general surgical practice. Now retired with four grown children, he lives in the town of Laurens.

Sheesley didn't fly again after the war. That was something he did for his country. He said the pressure the crews were under and their youth kept them going.

Dr. Byron Sheesley in his study at home in Laurens, surrounded by reminders of his flying days in World War II. (Photo by Julie Lewis)

"Nobody really realized what they were up against," he said. "We'd lose some planes, just about every time. Everybody looked at the other plane and thought 'We're going to miss you guys.' That's just about the way everybody felt. We just had a lot of hope, but still you'd be scared to death while you were doing it."

Survivors Of The Bulge

Area vets recall the cold and death in fighting Hitler's last-ditch offensive

Ed Keoughan

Ed Keoughan still remembers Christmas dinner 50 years ago: a hard, frozen chocolate bar in the midst of the Ardennes Forest. Landin Van Buren does, too: a turkey dinner that was scraped from the snow and reheated after the jeep carrying it was hit by a shell. But that was a rare, warm meal.

There was bitter cold and death for thousands in December of 1944.

That month, Adolf Hitler made a last, desperate attempt at winning World War II. The Allied armies had driven the Germans back from the coast of France and were advancing from both the west and the east.

But in a surprise attack in the early morning of Dec. 16, Hitler's forces smashed through the Ardennes Forest in northern Luxembourg and Belgium, creating a "bulge" in the Allies' western front.

Keoughan, staff sergeant of Company C with the 291st Engineer Combat Battalion, got word something was up on Dec. 15 with the report of German paratroopers dropping in the area. The Jefferson man was near the town of Sourbrodt, northeast of Malmedy, Belgium.

"We went and we searched the forests," he said. "We found some parachutes, but we didn't find any Germans. We come to find out that they were all dressed in American uniforms, they all spoke excellent English. And their job was to just upset behind the lines, change street signs and stuff like that." But the Allies didn't know that at the time.

As Waffen SS Colonel Jochen Peiper advanced, Keoughan's unit blew up a gas dump to thwart him, set up road blocks, lay mines, blew up bridges and built others. As a result, Peiper was later heard cursing "the damned engineers."

To the north, Landin Van Buren was near Aachen, Germany, by the Belgian border when the battle started. He and other members of the 84th Infantry Division were moved to Belgium's city of Marche Dec. 20 and told to hold it, helping prevent the Germans' goal of crossing the Meuse River and driving on to Antwerp. Members of rifle Company A, they were sometimes on the front lines.

Battle of the Bulge veterans Landin Van Buren, Ed Keoughan, and Howard Etts gather around the grave of Clifford Beers, a Davenport serviceman who was killed during the battle and is buried in Davenport Cemetery. (Photo by Julie Lewis)

Keoughan's unit called to duty after slaughter of U.S. troops in Malmedy

On Dec. 17, 1944 Ed Keoughan of Jefferson was about about a mile down the road outside Malmedy, Belgium with other members of Company C Combat Engineers of the 291st Battalion in World War II.

They didn't know it then, but about 150 men in the 285th Field Artillery Observation Battalion were surprised by a German armored column on another road, coming under heavy fire. Unprotected by tanks or heavy weapons, the Americans quickly surrendered.

As most of SS Colonel Jochen Peiper's panzers continued on, the unarmed American prisoners were herded into a nearby field by members of the First SS Panzer Division. Remembered as one of the war's atrocities, at about 2 p.m. a pistol shot rang out, followed by machine gun fire, which left at least 85 Americans lying dead in the snow. The survivors, shocked and wounded, made it to Malmedy that night.

Some time elapsed before it was safe to retrieve the bodies. Keoughan's Company C was given the job.

"They had put some booby traps and mines with the bodies, that's why they called the engineers back. That was our job, booby traps," Keoughan said, recalling the time with emotion. "We had to dig all the guys out of the snow and load them in trucks."

News of the massacre spread widely and helped stiffen American resolve to win the war. Later, the 291st Engineer Combat Battalion received the Croix de Guerre with Silver Star from the French government, for distinguishing itself in a remarkable manner in Belgium.

Battalion members also received a Presidential Unit Citation for outstanding performance of duty from Dec. 17 to 26, 1944, in Belgium.

"At one of our reunions, the colonel asked me 'Ed, What do you think made our outfit such a good outfit?' And I said, 'Colonel, there was only one thing and that was faith,'" Keoughan said. "We had faith in God, faith in country, and more than that, we had faith in each other."

"My particular battalion was assigned a hill on the outside of the city," the Oneonta man said. "We attempted to dig foxholes on that hill, but the ground was frozen and it was very difficult to dig in. And we didn't really know where the front was."

After a few days and sporadic attacks on the division, Staff Sergeant Van Buren led a patrol into the deserted city to see if they could spot the enemy.

"There was one three-story building in town, so I said to the men, 'Let's go up to the top floor where we can get up higher and take a look.'" They were just in time to see a column of German tanks coming up the road toward the city.

Leaving by the back door and crossing snowy fields, they reported back to their unit and kept their defensive position. There was fire on both sides of them as the Germans advanced, but not on them. The battle raged on, and after the new year his regiment was assigned to the 2nd Armored Division and took the offensive.

Landin Van Buren

"The first day of the attack, on that Jan. 3, was one of the days it started snowing hard," said Van Buren, who was later awarded a Bronze Star for service beyond the call of duty. "In a matter of just a very few hours that morning, the tanks got so they couldn't move at all. There was ice and snow on the roads — they just sat there and spun their tracks."

Snow mounted from knee- to waist-deep. At times near-blizzard conditions were the enemy, with temperatures hovering about 10 to 15 degrees. Although he had an extra pair of socks that he changed twice a day, putting the wet ones inside his shirt to dry out, Van Buren and many others suffered frostbitten or frozen feet.

"The shoes that we had were the regular combat boots — just leather boots," he said. "The army had what they called snow packs, but they weren't delivered to us until a couple of weeks after the Bulge was over. They were waterproofed, like a hunting boot."

South of the Ardennes in the Alsace-Lorraine region of western France, Howard Etts was in the 800th Ordinance Co. with the Army's 100th Infantry Division when the surprise attack came.

"We were what they call a gypsy outfit," said Etts, who now lives in Dunraven, near Margaretville. "Some days we were in the lines; we could always tell how close we were by the angle of the artillery guns. If they were up like this, you knew you were close," he said, holding his hand at a 70-degree angle.

His company's primary job was servicing the trucks, half-tracks and jeeps, changing clutches, gassing up trucks and finding extra parts.

"Sometimes we worked under a tarpaulin, where they couldn't see the lights at night," he said. But most harrowing was repairing spades on Howitzers under fire during the battle.

"The spades on the 155s and the 105s were breaking 'cause the ground was frozen," Etts said. "They got the arc generator up there and put a cover over top of the whole thing so they wouldn't see the flash — 'cause any time (the Germans) would see the flash, you'd get shot at."

Trained as infantry, eight men from his unit were drafted for the front lines when they were

Howard Etts

needed. As sergeant, Etts served as the 50-caliber turret gunner in the lead vehicle when the unit moved. The unit received a Presidential Unit Citation, with five men in his company receiving Bronze Stars.

There were 81,000 American casualties in the Bulge, including 19,000 men killed. The Germans advanced 60 miles through Luxembourg and Belgium, but stalled 65 miles short of Antwerp when the battle ended on Jan. 25, 1945.

All three of the men say that the worst was the cold and the lack of hot food. Many went for a month without changing clothes, slept with boots in their sleeping bags so they wouldn't freeze, and curled up in foxholes, or anywhere they could. Some went for a month without sleeping indoors.

"Most winters I enjoy, but last winter I did not because it reminded me too much of the Bulge," said Van Buren, who had flashbacks last year. "I finally said, 'I'm going to take a motor home and get out of here.'"

Veteran finds common bond to Belgium

As a combat engineer of the 291st Engineer Battalion with the U.S. 1st Army, Ed Keoughan and his platoon were charged with defense of Engineer Combat Group headquarters, set up in the town of Trois-Ponts, Belgium. The troops stayed there for a month in the autumn of 1944.

"We got to know all the people in Trois-Ponts; the man that ran the jewelry store," said Keoughan, who now lives in the town of Jefferson. "We stayed in the hotel and got to know those people — in fact, we ate with them. The mayor would have us down to his house for dinner, and all that kind of thing. It was really, really nice."

During October, troop headquarters moved and Keoughan returned to his battalion to help build Bailey assault bridges and help with winter defenses in other parts of Belgium. The town was later bombed, with much of it destroyed.

Imagine his surprise this fall, to meet a Rotary Exchange Student from Trois-Ponts, who is attending Stamford Central School this year. But, if he was astounded, she was more so.

"It made the world seem much smaller," said Pascale Bairin, who is 18. "To meet someone that came from my town, in America. Wow."

The town they both know wasn't their only bond. Bairin's grandparents also had first-hand experience with the Germans.

"Our grandparents all the time told us about the war, and it's really strong for them," she said. "My grandfather had to hide from the Germans. The SS were seeking for him because he had no (legal) identity and they wanted him to work for them.

"But he didn't want to, so he ran away. He lived in the woods during the night, to hide himself," she said. "And he had to walk a long ways to get food."

Later, he wrote a book about what happened in that region during the war.

When they talked about Belgium, Bairin gave Keoughan a book "Battle of the Bulge: Memory Routes," which explains monuments to Allied soldiers and their deeds during the war. In turn, he gave her a book on his company's work in Trois-Ponts.

Bairin will be in Stamford, where she stays with Bob and Lynn Arno, until the end of July. She plans to travel across the U.S. before returning home.

"It was wonderful to meet him," she said. "If I see the monuments again in Belgium, I will pay attention to them more, since I met him."

Myrtie Light still has her Link Trainer Log Books. Smooth and tan, 5-by 7-inches, they're filled with names of men she talked to day by day. Men she trained to fly "blind," in case their lives depended on it. Men she would never see again.

Light was one of the thousands of women who volunteered for the military during World War II. She served behind the scenes in the Naval Reserve's Women Accepted for Volunteer Emergency Service from 1943-45.

After receiving a crash course herself, the Gilbertsville woman became a Link Trainer instructor, teaching pilots to fly by instrument.

"The Link Trainers were made in Binghamton," she said, looking over the log books in her living room. "They're still made, but they're more complicated."

The large "blue box" was a machine that simulated flying conditions, helping cadets learn how to fly in the dark. Light also taught radio range and direction finding, orientation and how to land on aircraft carriers.

"The whole purpose of the WAVES was to replace the men, so they could go into combat," she said. "When I went to Pensacola (Fla.), to Whiting Field, the men who had been doing that (instruction) left."

Not only were there American boys, but some from the Royal Navy Air Force and the Free French who came for training. After working with Light or another specialist technician, pilots were tested in the air on the same procedures before being sent to the South Pacific, she said.

The machines were the size of a desk, about three feet high and four or five feet long. One person could sit as if he were in a cockpit, with instruments before him. Light created hypothetical problems for the flyers to solve, to see if they could find their way back with instruments.

"There was a sound he would hear and if he was going the wrong way, it would get fainter and fainter," she said. "Then when he got close to the beam it made a big sound. When he got on the beam it would guide him in; the louder you got, the closer you were (to the landing point)."

Veterans Of The Home Front

Women helped keep military going as men left for war

Working seven days on and one day off, WAVES sometimes took a bus into Pensicola for relaxation. They wore grey seersucker dresses with ties in the summer and navy blue wool jackets and skirts during winter. They could, however, wear navy slacks with white shirts during training.

"They also had women who were servicing the planes there — mechanics," Light said. "And then they had control tower girls, air traffic controllers."

Later, Light served at naval air stations in the then-territory of Hawaii and remained there until the war ended in August of '45. She married veteran Eric Light in 1950, and both before and after the war taught elementary school.

Across the village of Gilbertsville is another behind-the-scenes veteran. Dorothy Feiser Chynoweth was a young teacher in Gilbertsville in 1942 when she filled out an application to join the new Women's Army Auxiliary Corps.

After her acceptance, Chynoweth went to Des Moines, Iowa, and joined the fifth officer can-

Myrtie Light in 1943.

Dorothy Chynoweth at her desk in the Army School at the Fort Des Moines, Iowa, WAAC Training Center in 1944.

70

didate class at the new WAAC Training Center there.

"When I reported, we still had men officers," she said. "The first (women) officers were just finishing their six-week training."

A former Cavalry post, Fort Des Moines had a parade ground surrounded by brick buildings that housed officers, along with renovated stables for enlisted women's quarters. Her first assignment after training was to teach others Army subjects at the school. She began with clerk duties and office management.

"I did that for some little time, until eventually I was in charge of the school for the enlisted women," she said. "There were about four different types of training that the enlisted women had: There were clerks, cooks and bakers, driver training — all these different things."

After a year in the Corps, the "Auxiliary" was dropped from the WAAC, and the Corps joined the regular Army. At that point, the women were given a choice whether to remain in service, which Chynoweth did. Rising to the rank of captain, she acted as principal of the Army school, guiding the approximately 200 women there.

World War II veterans Myrtie Light (left), and Dorothy Chynoweth recall their years in military service at Chynoweth's home. Both live in Gilbertsville. (Photo by Julie Lewis)

After two and a half years, she requested a transfer to Edgewood Arsenal, Md., a chemical warfare center, to be closer to family in New Jersey. After a year and a half in personnel work there, she left the Army in 1946.

Later she married, continuing her career teaching high school English, before retiring to Gilbertsville in 1981. She is now commander of the Gilbertsville American Legion Post 1339.

"The fellas got hold of me right away," Chynoweth said. "There were several of us who knew each other as children, so that I was friends of theirs. I like the Legion, because I think we contribute to the village quite a bit."

71

Former Scintilla workers Amy Baker (left), and Agnes Elliott stand in front of a gate of the Amphenol Corporation plant on Union Street in Sidney. (Photo by Julie Lewis)

They built the tools of war

Agnes Elliott remembers the factory windows painted black.

They hid the lights inside from possible enemy planes.

Living in Sidney with her sister in the early 1940s, Elliott worked at the Scintilla plant there, inspecting magnetos used in airplane ignitions.

She walked to work in her skirt and ankle socks, starting at 7 a.m.

"If you were out there and the whistle blew, you got in. And you had badges to get in with, with your picture on it or you couldn't get in," said Elliott, who now lives in New Berlin. "They had quite a few guards, just to be on the protective side."

Many factory workers commuted by bus from Binghamton, Norwich and Oneonta, since gasoline was rationed. They sat for long hours at benches, inspecting screws, nuts, bolts and cams for airplanes. Often it was tedious work.

"We took everything off the machines and inspected them right then," she said. "Sometimes you did the same thing over and over, sometimes you had little screws you had to look at under microscopes."

As 16 million Americans went off to fight in World War II, 10 million others took over their jobs. But, as the United States increased its war production to 40 percent of the economy by 1944, a new source of labor was tapped: women.

Millions went to work making bombs and airplane engines, working on ships and railways. The Scintilla plant in Sidney had been acquired by the Bendix Corp. which made flight guidance systems, electrical connectors and flight instruments before the war. It is now known as the Bendix Connector Operations of Amphenol Corporation.

Elliott had worked a five-day, 40-hour week at the factory since 1939.

"On Dec. 7, 1941, we got word that the Japanese had bombed us, and we worked 10 hours a day, seven days a week. We started right in, the next day," she said.

Guided by blueprints, she measured parts with micrometers and verniers, and threaded screws into larger units to make sure they worked.

On the cam line with her was Amy Baker of Norwich.

"They had a 'forelady' to keep the work up to the benches for us," Baker said. "And over her was a foreman and over that was a supervisor" within the Small Parts Inspection department. "This was in a really big room."

Starting at Scintilla in May of 1940, Baker worked until 1944 when she left to have twins in her late 20s.

"They set up lines where they made cams from blocks, from the beginning — with a machine, all the way up through, sometimes just from raw material," she said. It became a real assembly line.

Good parts were sent to the Stock Department, while others were sent back to be reworked, Baker said.

As increasing numbers of men left for the war, women took over jobs such as running drill presses.

"I don't think the women got to work down on the big machines, where it first started the cam from scratch," she said. "We lost inspectors, the men, and we had more or less women on the machines working and then we had about six inspectors, I think, looking at the (finished) parts as they come up through. We had two men there."

Baker was later promoted to a line inspector, checking quality of the parts each step of the assembly. She was also in charge of her inspection bench, supervising six or eight others.

"It was an awful sad period, too," Elliott said. "You'd see all these young fellas there and the next thing you knew, they had gone out."

Although most men had left the factory, they weren't forgotten. Flags hung in the departments, with a star representing each man in the armed services. Yet even patriotism had its dark side.

"We had either one or two Japanese families at that time, working in there. And they were made to leave Bendix," Elliott said. "They lived right in Sidney. They were a good family, too — there was just the fear of them, I guess."

The High Cost For Iwo Jima

Area 'Seabees' followed first waves to hit the island

Theodore DeMyttenaere

As he stepped off his landing craft, Theodore DeMyttenaere saw the first wave of Marines ahead of him on the beach. It was Feb. 19, 1945. The island was Iwo Jima.

As a petty officer with the 133rd Naval Construction Battalion, his group was attached to the 4th Marine Division invading the Pacific island.

"We came in between the first and second waves," he said. "You didn't have much time to look around, you had to do what your job was. We unloaded boxes and trucks from Higgins craft, and one of them was a communications outfit with telephone line and all that kind of stuff."

DeMyttenaere and others in his 1,100 battalion slung 45 caliber Thompson submachine guns over their backs on a strap, as they unloaded ammunition for the assaulting Marines. Bulldozers left landing craft to clear away rocks, but some trucks became mired in the soft, black sand. And all around him there was noise and pain.

"There were a lot of explosions — mortar shells, mostly," he said slowly, looking across his living room in North Franklin. "A lot of guys got hit. In our outfit, when they ended up being counted, there 356 that were either hurt or killed."

For three or four days his construction battalion, or Seabees, kept up its support, unloading and moving supplies.

"We didn't have time to think about getting rested; we didn't get any sleep," he said. "You had rations for three days in your pack. You got up anywhere you could get, to eat. The Japanese were up on top — one side was really quite steep."

"Seabees" was the name given to the Navy's newly established construction battalions, which underwent military and construction training, then followed the Marines ashore. Not meant as offensive groups, the Seabees could still defend themselves if needed.

For 75 days before the assault on the 8-square-mile island, American bombers from Saipan and naval guns had "softened up" Iwo Jima. On the morning of Feb. 19, the largest group of ships used in a Pacific operation until then collected offshore — 450 vessels of the U.S. Fifth Fleet.

Meanwhile, the 4th and 5th Marine Divisions with 30,000 men invaded the volcanic-ash beaches in what became the bloodiest operation in the history of the U.S. Marine Corps.

Wounded when a mortar shell exploded beside him, DeMyttenaere was temporarily paralyzed from the waist down and spent five days on a hospital ship and three days at a Saipan medical area. When the paralysis passed, he asked to go back to his outfit.

About that time Dr. Harry Wilbur of Walton was arriving on Iwo Jima.

"We landed on what they called Blue Beach, better known to people there as All Blew to Hell Beach," he said. "We went on over to White Beach for a temporary encampment, and that's where this banzai attack came.

"There was a company of Marines in the middle of the night that were to go down to the landing craft and go to Okinawa, and these Japanese fell in right behind them, figuring that they would go down and surprise them and take over the ship and get back to Japan," he said. "They ended up in a Seabee compound."

More than a month after the initial invasion, many Japanese still hid in tunnels and caves on the pork chop-shaped island.

"Talk about Swiss cheese; there were caves all over the place, and they were holed up in them," Wilbur said. It was later learned that the entrenched Japanese force numbered 21,000 men in an 11-mile maze of bombproof underground hideouts and camouflaged pillboxes.

In the early morning hours of March 26, 1945, it was Wilbur's 90th Construction Battalion that was the site of the banzai, or suicidal, attack.

"The officers all had to sleep above ground in tents; the men could sleep in foxholes, if they could make them. Well, here was a brand-new tent and I was in there, and all of a sudden I could hear all this shooting and banging and everything else, and I didn't know what was going on at first," he said at his home.

"Then there was a 'pffft' and I saw light where a bullet had gone through the tent. I was so doggone scared, I didn't know whether to roll off the cot onto the ground or not."

About 240 Japanese were killed in the resulting fight, and Wilbur and other medical officers tended patients in the 90th Sick Bay. Two men from the 90th were killed, and some others were wounded. Having finished his medical training in December 1943, Wilbur was a Navy lieutenant junior grade 50 years ago, at age 29. He has now been Delaware County medical examiner for nearly 43 years.

In spite of ongoing bombing, the Seabees built permanent camps, barber shops and post offices. But perhaps their biggest project was airfields. While Wilbur tended health problems at regular sick call hours, DeMyttenaere worked crushing rock and building roads, to join the three existing Japanese airstrips into one.

But before building roads, they had to remove mines.

"We had a steel rod about 3 feet long and about 3/8 to a 1/2-inch in diameter," DeMyttenaere said. "You lay on the ground and put the steel rod in front of you, and you had about 3 foot in width, and somebody else had about 3 foot and you covered the ground.

"They were metal mines and you'd feel it through the sand. There was a half a circle and they had two or three long nobs on them, sticking up, and if you hit one of them you blew it up. If that happened, you'd be gone."

The sand could be brushed away, the mine dug up and set beside the road with others. They were picked up and put on trucks, then taken away to be detonated, he said. The cleared road was marked with a tape held down by sand.

"If you went off the road, it was just tough luck," DeMyttenaere said.

Securing the island was a victory, allowing P-51 Mustang fighters to escort a daytime bombing raid on Tokyo by April 7. In addition, by holding Iwo Jima, more than 2,200 damaged B-29 bombers landed during five months, saving the lives of nearly 25,000 airmen.

But the cost was extremely high. By the end of March, 6,821 Americans had been killed, 5,453 of them Marines, and almost 18,000 wounded. More than 18,000 Japanese defenders died there.

On March 14, Iwo Jima — "Hell with the fire out " — was declared secure. After Japan's surrender in August many on the island, including Wilbur and DeMyttenaere, went on as occupation forces.

Dr. Harry Wilbur of Walton holds a rock from Iwo Jima into which he carved his battalion's name 50 years ago. Beside him is a suitcase he made from a wing of the first Japanese "Betty" that bombed Americans on Iwo Jima. In front is an ashtray he made from part of the plane's propeller.(Photo by Julie Lewis)

Local sailor's ship bombed beaches for the Marines

The night was inky black.

Water lapped the side of the ship as the radio request came through.

Japanese troops on Iwo Jima were massing for a suicide attack and U.S. Marines needed help.

Fire support moved in from the sea, in the shape of the USS *Henry A. Wiley*, one of 12 destroyer minelayers built by the Navy during World War II. Charles Nichols of Oneonta was mount captain of the secondary battery on the *Wiley*, directing the crews that operated two guns.

"Using radar, of course, we got in position. Guys swear they could hear the bow scraping on the beach — that's how close we were," he said. "Then they said 'illuminate,' and we said, they'll blow us out of the water with that search light on."

But the Marines knew what they needed, so as the search light from the ship swept the coastline, all the ship's guns fired where the light shone in a sweep.

Charles Nichols

"It all happened at once, like the most wild Fourth of July fireworks you ever saw in your life — just zap! All we saw were the enemy's fannies going over rocks," Nichols said. "Then cease fire, the scene is ended, the curtain dropped. It was inky black again."

Marines nicknamed the Wiley "Hammering Hank" that night for its work knocking back the Japanese. As a fire support ship for Marines on Red Beach at the base of Mount Suribachi, the *Wiley* was directed by the Marine's fire control party on the beach.

"They called the shots, and we went in and did it," Nichols said. "We were there every day for about four days. We would leave the area for logistics — go back and get more ammunition, more fuel, then come back in — usually we did that at night time."

As part of the pre-invasion bombardment group, the ship arrived on Feb. 16 with other fighting vessels, blasting at the island from dawn until dark, Nichols said.

"Each of us had areas that we saturated with gunfire, to soften up the beach areas prior to the invasion," he said, noting that at first the Japanese would only fire back once in a while. "They were very cagey. They didn't want you to learn where their heavy guns were located. When a heavy gun fires, it leaves a smoke burst; then you can target in on it."

The USS Henry A. Wiley at its homecoming into San Francisco Bay, February 17, 1946. One of 12 destroyer minelayers ever built by the Navy, its crew saw their first fighting at Iwo Jima.

With its 5-inch, 40-mm, 20-mm and 50-caliber shells pumping, Nichols' ship destroyed 23 heavy gun implacements, including several large mortars. As mount captain, Nichols wore earphones, communicating with the director tower and relaying messages to his gun crews of five men each.

The *Wiley* narrowly escaped an attack from an 8-inch cannon on Iwo Jima, and later repelled more than 60 kamikaze attacks off Okinawa, destroyed 15 enemy planes and two Baka bombs. The ship's crew earned four battle stars and the Presidential Unit Citation with Star.

"You never can really 100 percent relax, and yet you try to relax as best you can," Nichols said. "You shoot the baloney, smoke a cigarette, have a pot of coffee, tell sea stories and act nonchalant, when inside you're all tensed up."

Yet in spite of this tension, or because of it, an unbreakable camaraderie develops among sailors.

"It's a bond that you develop that even blood relatives don't have," Nichols said. "It's because he puts his life on the line every day for you, and you in turn do the same for him. That bond develops a feeling of fidelity that can't be changed throughout time.

"In fact, at our reunions now when they close up our banquet we stand and shake the hand of the guy on our right and our left and thank them that we're there. Because if it wasn't for him, I wouldn't be here."

War Brides Redefine 'Home'

Stella Hobbs from Kintbury had borrowed a wedding dress, as many English girls did in the early 1940s. Most people didn't buy extras during World War II.

Still, she didn't get to wear it. When plans she'd made to marry American Fred Koerner in a church fell through, she travelled to where he was stationed with the U.S. Army in Blackpool, marrying him there before the Allied invasion of France.

"We were supposed to be married in April, but he had to have permission to marry, from the American government," said Stella Koerner, who lives with Fred in the town of Milford. "And, of course, they checked on my background. We had piles of paper."

After applying for permission in January 1944, they planned to marry on her mother's silver wedding anniversary. When the papers hadn't arrived by then, they had to postpone the wedding until May and she was married in her black travel suit.

The couple met at an English fair in Newbury the previous summer.

"My girlfriend and I were the only girls on the electric bumping cars," she said. "It was all full with American soldiers. We met up, and we've been together ever since."

Even before coming to the United States, a war bride's club formed in Newbury as a support network for English women who had married Americans in the armed services. Koerner still has a group photo of 34 war brides.

"We used to get together, I think it was once a month. And there were these two American girls, and they would talk to us and tell us things about what to expect. Some of them were my friends; I mean, we grew up together. Some of them I worked with. I kept in touch with two or three of them, but over the years we've drifted apart," she said.

Although Fred Koerner came from Iowa, upon his discharge in December 1945 he came and joined his mother, Cora, in Oneonta. His new wife arrived at age 20 on March 28, 1946.

"I liked it very much when I got here. The only thing I couldn't understand was how any-

Charles and Lucette Wolfe in September 1945.

Born Lucette Biermann in Normandy, France, she moved to Paris as a girl and was 13 when World War II broke out in 1939. By November 1944 she was a young working woman and Charles Wolfe served with the U.S. Army's Military Police in Paris.

"He was an MP at a hospital gate, and to take my bus to go to work, I had to go there," she said. "He had a dictionary and we would talk that way," she said.

They fell in love, and by September of '45 when he got orders to leave for home from Marseilles, they wanted to remain together.

"We really didn't intend to get married then, but my mother wouldn't let me go, otherwise," she said. So, on Sept. 7, 1945 the Wolfes were married in a simple civil ceremony — twice.

"We got married by the Army chaplain, after being married by the French justice in the courthouse," said Lucette Wolfe. "The American and French governments saw that all the paperwork was done. They were taking no chances that women would be married and left behind, some even with little ones, which happened after the first war."

body knew what land belonged to everybody, because nothing gets separated," Stella Koerner said. "We always had hedgerows."

Although she was homesick, her mother-in-law was kind and helped her adjust to her new country.

"I didn't like the food; everything tasted different to me because of the way it was fixed," she said. "When I came here I weighed about 160 pounds and I went down to just over 100 pounds in about four months. It's just like, if you buy beef that's raised in another area, it has a different flavor to it. Eating was my main trouble."

Lucette Wolfe had a different problem: She couldn't read the packages in American grocery stores.

Fred and Stella Koerner in May 1944.

Stella Koerner (left) and Lucette Wolfe, sit in Koerner's living room in the town of Milford with a chair and trunk she brought from England after marrying an American soldier during World War II. (Photo by Julie Lewis)

Charles Wolfe was discharged in December 1945 and his new wife arrived in New York City on March 21, 1946. They lived in Oneonta before he took up farm work and they bought Stone House Farm in Mount Vision in 1949. Through reading and practice, she taught herself English.

"It was different to me because I come from the city, one of the biggest in the world — this was like the back woods," Lucette said. "The hardest part was leaving your country and your family. We wrote, but it was very, very expensive to call at that time."

Still, the women's ties to their homelands have never broken. The Wolfes, who now live in Oneonta, have been back to France several times, and Lucette has a sister who comes here. They have two grown sons now, and grandchildren.

Koerner's sister and brother are still in England, and the family visits back and forth. She wouldn't live anywhere other than here, she said, although she referred to England as "home."

The Koerners' roots here run deep, as well. They have two sons in the area and a daughter in Utah. Fred made a career with the Delaware & Hudson Railroad and Stella kept at least one continuity across the Atlantic.

She worked at Woolworth's "tea bar" restaurant in Newbury before emigrating, and then at Bresee's Health Bar for 28 years in Oneonta.

Brides follow husbands to safety

Francine Payne, age 8.

As well as the love they shared with their new husbands, foreign war brides found another benefit by moving to the United States: safety. And, though they have been on safer ground for nearly 50 years, Hitler's terrorization of European nations and Great Britain still affects some of them today.

"When I hear sirens from fire trucks, I still get goose pimples because it has the same piercing effect that the (air raid) sirens had. It's that quickness; you go like that," said Stella Koerner, looking startled, "and you feel that tension come up. I think it's just something you never outgrow."

Children were evacuated from heavily-bombed London into the countryside and even sent to Canada. A girl from London lived with Koerner's family in Kintbury, south of London, in the early 1940s. Everyone, including children, was given a gas mask.

It was also common to build large cupboards under stairways, to hide in, and to dig areas outside the house for bomb shelters.

"To this day, I have claustrophobia — I can't stand being shut up anywhere," said Koerner, who lives in Milford.

Francine Savory also remembers hiding. Her mother, the late Olga Maria Payne, was an Englishwoman who married an American in 1945. The second marriage for both parents, Francine was 8 years old when she and her mother joined Bill Payne in Bainbridge in March of 1946.

"He was a member of the CID, Criminal Investigation Division, in the Army, stationed in Europe," Savory said at her home in Sidney. "Our relatives over here asked him to look my mother and I up ... to see how we'd survived the war."

Her grandparents ran a big Italian restaurant in London, where Bill Payne and other servicemen went, and though Olga worked as a model in

Francine Savory of Sidney holds a photo of her mother, who married an American. (Photo by Julie Lewis)

the city she helped out her parents in the restaurant — and met Payne.

At that time, Savory attended a Catholic school in the small town of Hendon, where they lived outside London.

"We had a big air raid shelter, a bomb shelter, in the kitchen of this house," she said. "We would use it like a kitchen table and everything, but it was all mesh around the outside, with the opening in it and we kept all the food under there and the blankets and everything. But one end was built out a little bit, so you could sit and eat around it."

Approximately 10 by 12-feet, the shelter was big enough for the two of them to sleep in. It was made of metal, with the top a heavy reinforced steel.

"(My mother) often wondered, had we dove in there and a bomb had hit the house and collapsed on us, how we ever would have gotten out. But you didn't think about that at the time."

No matter where they were, when sirens went off, people acted. Maps in the "underground" or subway, showed the site of the nearest shelter and air raid wardens on the streets of London gave directions.

"If you were at the convent (school), you had a drill to go to the nearest bomb shelter and you had to stay there till the 'all-clear' sounded," Savory said. "If you were on the streets, there were bomb shelters all over; you ran for cover to the nearest one. And you just literally held your breath."

Savory's brother, John Payne, was born here in 1947, but their mother never returned to England.

"She left her mother over there, and her sister over there and a brother-in-law and two nephews, and she said she could never, ever go back and say good-bye again," she said. As an adult, Savory has returned to England twice, one time taking her son, Michael.

Olga and Bill Payne in June 1945.

There were enough women in the tri-towns area to form a "war bride's club" after they arrived. There were women who had come from England, Belgium and France, who met monthly and talked about adjusting to America.

Now 57, Savory said that coming to the United States as a girl she felt both excitement and relief.

"I guess I was so scared and the most of my life that I could remember was the war," she said. "To me, it was a safe haven. I just saw it as a whole new adventure with peace — it was exciting. And to have a father." The late Bill Payne was a member of the Bainbridge Police Department and served as chief for many years.

On the other hand, people got so used to the bombing, that at times they became almost callous to the danger. Stella Koerner recalls being in an industrial area near London, when her husband heard explosions in the distance.

"We went up to visit my sister, and Fred said, 'They're dropping bombs, I can hear them' and I said 'That's all right, they're way over there.' You have no fear of it, I think, after a while," she said. "You're so used to it, you just live with it. He still kids me about it."

Entering The Gates Of Hell

Oneonta native confronted horror of concentration camp

Al Hough burns a Nazi flag outside SS troop living quarters in Kirn, Germany, in April 1945.

There was nothing that could have prepared him. In spite of the years he'd fought the Germans in Africa and France, Al Hough never expected the sights that filled his eyes near the end of World War II. Stepping into a concentration camp, he entered the gates of hell.

A group of men shot right before his arrival lay dead. Investigating the camp barracks, Hough and other troops found that prisoners too weak to walk had been shot lying in their meager wooden bunks. His group found one man alive.

"It was a cruel, very cruel thing. And the smell of burned flesh and stuff there was terrible," he said. Later he found out that SS guards had killed the prisoners.

With the 89th Infantry Division in France, he had fired his way into Germany. In April 1945, the Oneonta native and other members of the Rolling W Cannon Company worked their way across Germany toward the Mulde River, "mopping up" as the Nazis retreated. Before that, he was wounded serving with the Army's 1st Division in the 18th Infantry.

A few camp inmates who weren't too weak stayed to explain the site to the soldiers. Hough saw whipping tables where prisoners were tied and beaten with long wooden dowels. A movable gallows was used in a central area for public hangings after prisoners committed an offense.

Even more gruesome, if possible, were boxes holding teeth with gold fillings from the dead and rings taken from their fingers.

"At one place they had rows of railroad ties with bodies in between and they were partially burned; it was an awful smell," Hough said at his home in the town of Maryland. "They were piled up and there was dirt with them. They had burned, and were trying to get rid of the bodies — I guess that was it. They had a crematorium there, too."

But the war in Europe was almost over.

Hough often went with several others as runners to contact other companies, after telephone lines had been cut.

"The first that I knew there was a prison camp (nearby), we were in this little town and I saw all these German prisoners — they had been German prisoners — in their striped suits," Hough said. "They had their hands on (each other's) shoulders and they were weak. They were walking away from this camp."

Al Hough of Maryland holds his medals from World War II campaigns and Nazi armbands confiscated during the war. (Photo by Julie Lewis)

They were outside the town of Ohrdruf, about 85 miles north of Nuremberg. Riflemen from the 89th had liberated a concentration camp and Hough's unit was right behind them.

"These people were so hungry, that they would see crackers that were stepped on, in the mud, and would gather them up and eat them, with the mud and all. I saw prisoners go over to a dung heap and get old potato peelings that we wouldn't think about eating — we wouldn't even give them to the pigs — that they went and got and ate, because they were so hungry," he said.

Prisoners were of many nationalities; Hough knows there were Czechs, Jews, a couple of Americans and probably others within the fence. A history of the 89th Infantry published by the U.S. military right after the war, includes the following:

"A search disclosed nearly 3,000 bodies burned and buried in pits north of the camp. A group of German citizens, by order of Army authorities, were made to witness these horrors — the whipping block, gallows, crematorium. No member of the 89th doubted Nazi barbarism after Stalag Ohrdruf."

Shortly after that, when Germany surrendered unconditionally on May 7, 1945, Hough was in a town outside Chemnitz, Germany, where his maternal grandfather had grown up.

"We stayed out in the fields, mostly. These people would walk out of the bushes; you'd be there and all of a sudden they'd appear," he said.

Al Hough, with other soldiers, beyond bodies found at a concentration camp outside Ohrdruf, Germany, in 1945.

"They knew it was safe and they were begging for food."

In addition, German soldiers sometimes gave themselves up, even those still armed — as long as no SS troops were in sight.

"They didn't dare, if the SS were around, because if the SS saw them they would shoot them," he said. "The SS were the ones that did the cruel things. I still dislike them. And it bothers me a great deal to hear that we have skinheads in this country who are following the Nazi path, because there's a danger there.

"This man that came down from Canada and was preaching that there was no such thing as this happening, is the only reason I'm telling you this. I'm not telling it because I like to do it. I'm trying to write about the war and it's difficult — my emotions get in there."

After living through such day-to-day fear, when victory was realized in Europe, relief mingled with the nagging knowledge that the war wasn't over, yet.

"Our officer came through and told us that the war was over, just like that," Hough said. "We had been fighting and we were all geared up — and boom, it's all over."

As his unit prepared to ship back to France, Hough had some contact with German civilians, who treated him well.

"The French would never give us any hot water or anything. They'd give us wine, but they wouldn't give us water," he said, noting that in contrast, a German man approached the GIs one morning with a kettle of hot water for shaving.

"They were friendly with us, because a lot of them were not with this movement at all. But they had no guns, they had no protection; they could not resist. If they did, off with their heads."

Soon after Germany's surrender, Hough's unit was back in France.

"We were supposed to then go to Japan," he said. "But our friendly president dropped the A-bomb and it ended it. Everybody hollers what a cruel thing it was, but it wasn't cruel to me because I knew what we were in for. Having people from my family who were over that way, we knew that that was no picnic, either."

Another area soldier in Germany then was Robert Knight. A member of the Army's 82nd Airborne Division, he was a glider trooper who served in the campaigns for Sicily, Italy, Normandy and Holland. He was at the Elbe River on May 3 when the 21st German Army surrendered to his division.

Knight, who now lives on East Street in Oneonta, was billeted near the city of Ludwigslust, northwest of Wittenberg, for several weeks after Germany's surrender. Four miles north of the town of 10,000 was a concentration camp. A

V-E Day issue of a U.S. military newspaper contains photos of the camp's conditions and articles explaining that 700 inmates were hospitalized right after liberation; 57 died the first day.

"They made them bring 100 (bodies) into Ludwigslust and the German civilians — anyone that was there — had to walk all by them," Knight said. Five Wehrmacht generals and many other German officers were forced to join. Citizens dug graves for 200 slave laborers who had recently died at the camp — one of about 520 concentration camps and subcamps across occupied Europe.

"Things were very normal after that," he said. "Two or three hundred men and women from the prison camp got married in a mass marriage and the (U.S. military) band played for their wedding. A bunch of us were brought up ethnically anyway, so we played polkas and waltzes for a long time. And the liquor that we found was shared."

Most of the troops were elated, Knight said, expecting to go home soon, since they'd served in so many campaigns. By August he was on his way back to his wife, Bernie, in the States.

For years he taught at Delaware Academy, then was asked to teach music at the University of Augsburg in Germany from 1977 to 1989.

"I was a bit squeamish until the first week I was there," he said. "But by the time we came home, we saw more on television about the Holocaust, than any of you have ever seen every week. They've had actual footage (of the atrocities) on German television."

Knight was equally impressed by a trip to the infamous concentration camp at Dachau. "It's all there in black and white, and they've got the amount of people (who were killed.) And the S.O.B.s that say it never happened — all they have to do is go there and see. It's very low-key. The day we were there, there were mostly German people going through it.

"We got to meet other people our age who were in the war, and they were very blunt about it, too," he said. "One German chap that we know was, I think, 15 when they said 'You're in the army.' The first generation after that have such a guilty conscience, a lot of them."

Robert Knight of Oneonta holds a military newspaper printed on V-E Day, May 8, 1945. (Photo by Julie Lewis)

Events unfolded as home front watched

The end was coming.

Millions at home in the United States knew it, as did the soldiers across Europe and sailors off the coasts. Nazi Germany was about to fall.

As World War II entered its final painful months, Allied progress was daily front-page news. Dramatic events unfolded in The Oneonta Star as the Third Reich, Hitler's mad dream to "last a thousand years" unraveled.

The Oneonta Star's V-E Day extra on Monday, May 7, 1945.

On May 4, 1945 the Germans surrendered Denmark, Holland and all of northern Germany. However, they still occupied Norway.

May 5 German Army Group G, which included two armies, gave up near Munich.

Czechoslovakians still battled Nazis in Prague.

May 6 the U.S. Third Army captured the Bohemian arms center of Pilsen. And, in the wee hours of the morning on May 7, 1945 Germany surrendered unconditionally to the Allied armies at Rheims, France.

Fran Green of West Oneonta was a junior at Oneonta State Teacher's College.

"I got up that morning of the 7th and a friend of mine and I were talking," she said. "We had been told that when (victory) came through, we would have a day off. There was an anticipation."

Each day that week her friend had asked Green if she thought surrender would come that day, and on May 7 Green answered yes for a private reason — it was her birthday.

"Later on she came and saw me. I hadn't heard a radio, but she had at lunchtime," said Green, who also works as a historian at Huntington Memorial Library. "She looked me straight in the eye with tears streaming down her face and said 'Happy Birthday.'"

An extra edition of the Star that day ran a three-inch headline 'GERMANY QUITS' and a picture of Supreme Allied Commander, Gen. Dwight D. Eisenhower. Britain proclaimed May 8 Victory in Europe Day and London erupted in jubilation. President Harry S. Truman urged the American public to celebrate soberly, with prayer, as there was still much work to be done combating the Japanese.

"It wasn't the hoopla that happened in August. It was subdued," Green said. "People were relieved who had husbands and brothers and fathers in Europe."

Flying above the trees of Indochina, C. Wesley Coddington kept watch from the tail of his plane. As an armorer aboard the B-25 bomber, his job was to load and fuse the bombs before they dropped, and open the bomb hatch for the pilot.

"I had a pair of twin 50-caliber machine guns in the tail, and I was on my knees all the time," he said at his home in Otego. "I had a short seat that was at an incline ... but actually my weight was on my knees." This enabled him to see through a "bubble" window in the tail.

The battles fought against the Japanese in China, Burma and India have been called the forgotten wars. Yet, through the jungles, mountains and skies of the Asian theater, Allied soldiers struggled as others did on the slopes of Europe and the Pacific islands.

The B-25s were low-flying bombers, smaller than the B-17s and B-24s used at higher altitudes. Coddington's crew consisted of a pilot, engineer, navigator, radioman and himself. The plane held 14 machine guns and there was a 75 mm cannon in the nose, which fired shells almost two feet long.

"That was used, for instance, if we were called to take off a hilltop, or to take out shipping in the South China Sea or take a locomotive off a track. It was very destructive — and a wonderful piece of equipment, actually," he said.

Yet, flying at an average of between 500 and 13,000 feet, more B-25s were lost to enemy ground fire than in air fights. Returning from one flight, there were 132 holes in the bottom of Coddington's plane.

In fact, it was small arms fire that brought his plane down south of the Ledo Road in Burma in March of 1945. Two of the crew were killed and the bottom of the plane ripped out as it crashed into the jungle.

"We had to bury the two right there and then head generally north. It was jungle growth all the way through," he said. "We figured that we'd gone about three and a half miles and it took us almost seven days to do it."

The navigator had a compass, which guided them in the right direction, and the crew didn't meet any Japanese as they cut their way through foliage with knives. Lack of food became a problem, however.

Surviving The Jungle Raid

Flier recalls WWII China, Burma theater

Surrounded by photos of his wife, Virginia, his children and himself, C. Wesley Coddington holds photos of B-25 bombers in a hallway at his Otego home. (Photo by Julie Lewis)

tail position forward over the bomb bay to pull the pins from bombs and open the bay doors. With a fuel range of about 1,350 miles total, Coddington's targets were mostly railroads, shipping, personnel and bridges. The 14th Air Force, of which his 22nd Bomb Squadron was a unit, was documented for having knocked out 2,135 aircraft on the ground, 445 ships, 817 bridges and 1,225 locomotives.

Unlike in Europe, where 30 or 40 planes traveled together for bombing raids, in the China/Burma/India theater, or CBI, bombers often went out singly or in groups of two or three.

"It was an entirely different type of war," Coddington said. "Our targets were sporadic; they weren't condensed, in large cities. ... In Indochina, the supply route was railroads coming north, bringing the troops and supplies to the Japanese up north. It was up to us to stop this movement."

He enlisted on Dec. 7, 1942 and left with his crew for China in the spring of '43, taking a plane with them from stateside. The Japanese had cut the Burma Road in April 1942, severing China's overland supply route. The sole way to provide for Allied armies was by air, so what has been called one of the most spectacular airlifts of the war began: flying over the Himalayas from India to Burma and China.

"We were able to get our K rations out of the plane as best we could, and that lasted us three days," Coddington said. They drank from streams and ate a few berries before creating a makeshift camp at night.

"We cut branches and one would stay on duty and the others would sleep, and then we would change every two hours so somebody was on watch," he said. "Believe me, when you're there, you hear every crack and crinkle and you think somebody is there."

When they reached the Ledo Road, the men encountered a Red Cross unit, which helped them return to their barracks.

When it was time to drop a load during a bombing mission, Coddington crawled from his

"That was where we jumped over 'the Hump,'" Coddington said. "The Hump was where you had to travel anywhere from 15,000 to 27,000 feet in the air. We had to put oxygen on." There was only one flight route open over the mountains at that time, bringing supplies into Kunming, China.

Stationed in Yankai, China, Coddington took part in 29 missions. Fliers ate a rice-based diet cooked by Chinese allies, often with bamboo shoots, onions, garlic, and water buffalo for meat. Only at Thanksgiving did they get government rations.

When the monsoons began in August, bombing runs stopped for two to four months. The planes went out only when the weather cleared. The men played cards or took care of chores, such as servicing the aircrafts' machine guns.

One flight in particular Coddington doesn't like to recall, because it involved innocent animals.

"We had one horrible run one time when we had to bomb a corral of elephants. The story behind it is we kept taking out several bridges down in Indochina," he said. "And, within a couple of days the bridges would be back up again; or within operation, so that they could still have vehicles cross."

Intelligence learned that the Japanese were using elephants to pull logs into place across the river. The elephant area was found and Coddington's crew told to bomb it.

"It was probably one of the most horrible things that I've experienced," he said. "I'm an anti-cruelty to animals guy anyway."

Still, remembering flying 50 years ago, Coddington laughs to think how he loved the thrill of it as a 20-year-old. "Our pilot was a daredevil. He'd come up to a line of trees, come up all over them and come back down again," he said.

Mail call two or three times a week was the highlight of life in Yankai. Letters took two to three weeks from the States and packages took roughly three months. When family wrote ahead, asking what he'd like at Christmas, he stayed with the basics.

"I would just as soon have toilet paper and fruitcake," he said.

Under the command of Major General Claire L. Chennault, the 22nd Squadron was part of the 341st Bomb Group. Stationed in China, Americans worked with the Chinese underground, which supplied information about downed American planes through a network operating village-to-village in the countryside.

Coddington noted that he had a feeling of predestination, as far as survival was concerned. In the spring of '45, he became severely ill with dysentery, and later with malaria.

"The time I had dysentery, for instance, the fellow that took my spot in the plane because I could not fly, he never came back. And that was my spot," he said. "Things like that, you couldn't help but know and realize that the Lord had some reason."

C. Wesley Coddington (front row at right), poses with crew members and their B-25 bomber in Yankai, China in 1944. The plane's cannon is visible on the upper right.

Hiroshima At 50

Survivors recall the day that changed WWII – and history

Gordon Roberts

The Monday morning of Aug. 6, 1945, dawned clear and sunny over Hiroshima, Japan. At 8:16 the world changed forever when a four-ton atomic bomb shaped like a torpedo exploded 1,900 feet above the ground, near a bridge over the Ota River.

It was later estimated that the temperature directly beneath the explosion was at least 9,000 degrees F.

Between 80,000 and 100,000 people died instantly in the medium-size city.

That day has left the human race a haunting legacy: the creation of a ballooning nuclear arsenal, with enough deadly firepower to kill each man, woman and child on earth over and over again. The cloud from Hiroshima lingers with us still.

Now that 50 years have passed since that day during World War II, people around the globe are pausing to consider the ramifications, and recall the way they felt on that day. This is what they remember.

Gordon Roberts of Oneonta was a B-24 pilot stationed in China that year. A veteran of 66 bombing missions on Japanese supply and communication lines in northern China, he and his crew "lived by the bulletin board" where the flying schedule was posted.

"We got the notice 'They have dropped an atomic bomb on Hiroshima. The end of the war is close.' Naturally, we were relieved and thought we'd be able to go home," he said. "But, we didn't have any knowledge of the intensity of the bomb or how many people were killed."

Though Japan surrendered the following week, the war wasn't truly over for Roberts and his crew until October. To move planes and personnel out of China, many missions carrying gasoline had to be flown over the Himalayan Mountains — some in terrible weather that took lives. They didn't think too much about the atom bomb at the time, but there was a certain consensus.

"Most of the people of our generation felt that it was a terrible thing the way the war started at Pearl Harbor, with all the people killed with no warning," he said. "So there was the feeling that this sort of evened it up."

Ward Reynolds of Halcott Center served in the infantry in the South Pacific during 1942. Later he became a member of the 11th Airborne Division, training troops as glider infantry. He was training men in North Carolina when the atomic bomb was dropped.

"I thought it was a great thing; it saved lots of lives," he said. "Of course, there were lots of civilian lives lost."

His wife, Ruth, was a civilian member of the Women's Air Force Service Pilots, a group of more than 1,000 women in the Air Transport Command who flew planes to different sites in the U.S. From 1942-'44, she flew fighter and pursuit planes where needed.

"I had a brother in the crew of a B-29 in the Pacific," she said. "I guess I just about jumped up and down (when I heard). At that time, there was nobody as terrible and heinous as the Japanese."

Sugwon Kang holds a different view. Born and raised in Korea, where Japan was a colonial power, he grew up hating and fearing the Japanese. President Harry S. Truman, who helped liberate Korea from the Japanese, is somewhat of a national hero there. Truman also committed U.S. forces at the time of the Korean Conflict.

"In spite of those historical circumstances, I feel that the bomb was a terrible, terrible thing that he did," Kang said. "I feel now, more than ever before, that he should not have done it — it was cruel."

A professor of political science at Hartwick College in Oneonta, Kang has spent many days at the National Archives in Washington, D.C. studying diplomatic documents on the subject. He thinks the bomb dropped on Hiroshima, as well as the second one that hit Nagasaki on Aug. 9, were unnecessary, because Japan was already near collapse.

"It was a matter of days, possibly weeks, until they surrendered," Kang said. "We are talking about an enemy beaten, but now bowed."

He said with such a complex topic, one needs to realize the importance of the person who made the decision to use the bomb, Harry Truman.

"He has been praised, almost glorified, for being decisive," Kang explained. "Somebody else might have balked, somebody else might have had pangs of conscience before doing this. We are talking about cities, for God's sake, on completely helpless citizens." In addition, the technology to create the bomb had cost $1.8 billion, which may have been a factor in its use, he said.

Yet, the connection made between use of atomic weapons and the war's end is wrong, Kang said. U.S. forces were making such swift progress

Sugwon Kang

pushing the Japanese back to their mainland, that the war would have soon been over.

"Never mind how bad they were; they were beaten. If Japan was run by these fascist dictators, that's all the more reason not to punish the general population," Kang said. "Even General Eisenhower shook his head when he heard about it, saying it was totally unnecessary.

"I think the bomb should have been dropped on a military site for demonstration purposes, so they could see what we could do."

To complicate matters, the USSR declared war on Japan Aug. 8. Kang said the attack on Nagasaki was actually a message to the Russians to stay out of the war. The U.S. no longer needed their help to win.

This use of nuclear arms created the Cold War that followed. When the B-29 Enola Gay dropped the bomb dubbed "Little Boy" on Hiroshima, the U.S. demonstrated that nuclear weapons were acceptable at certain times. The Soviets and Chinese reacted by developing their own.

"I remember when the news broke out, and reading the reactions on faces of Korean grown-ups. I was a little boy at the time," Kang said. "We hated the Japanese. They were glad that the Japanese were being crushed, but they were also saying, 'My God, what kind of an age are we embarking on?'"

Otego man helped develop A-bomb

Chemist Robert Meeker got secret orders not long after he joined the Army in 1944, to travel to Oak Ridge, Tenn.

"As soon as I entered Oak Ridge, I had the sense that I was involved in something strange and different and exciting," said Meeker, a Colgate University graduate who now lives in Otego. "There were miles and miles and miles of board sidewalk and plywood shacks and buildings of various shapes and sizes — very little of a permanent nature. It looked like it had been put up overnight."

Robert Meeker of Otego holds his shirt that features an Army patch that depicts an atom being split. The patch was given for his research on the atomic bomb. (Photo by Julie Lewis)

Once there, the enlisted men were told that although they'd see and hear many strange things, they were not to tell anyone. In addition, their helmets and guns were collected since they were told they "wouldn't need them any more."

Meeker was part of the "Manhattan Project," a code name for the development and delivery of an atomic bomb.

"Oak Ridge was devoted to making uranium-235 isotope, which chemists thought could be made explosive if enough could be assembled," he said.

To that end, three factory-like plants had been built, with the U.S. Army Corps of Engineers in charge. Meeker worked in Lab 2 of the thermal diffusion plant, using Geiger counters to measure concentrations of the uranium-235 isotope, later used in the bomb dropped on Hiroshima.

Hundreds of civilians flocked to the area for work. Meeker's position was as a shift supervisor in charge of seven or eight civilian employees, all women. Another plant provided them with samples of uranium hexafluoride, a gas they called UF6.

"There was sort of an assembly line, using platinum hardware, because the UF6 is highly corrosive," he said. They repeatedly tested the uranium concentrations, passing hundreds of samples through the lab.

"Secrecy was paramount," he said. "The place was loaded with spies from Army intelligence, who were there in civilian clothes. There were also 'engineers' who weren't engineers at all, I found out later, but were intelligence," making sure no one talked about the research.

Months passed, and though Meeker knew what he was working with, he had no idea how it would be put to use, if efforts were successful. He thought it might be used with rifles, or to boost naval guns to expand their power — or be so devastating it would blow up an island.

"I'll never forget Aug. 6, 1945," he said. "I was working the 4 to 12 shift and listening to some music on a Knoxville station. I heard this voice say 'An atomic bomb was dropped on the Japanese city of Hiroshima early this morning. At this time, the extent of the damage is unknown, but is expected to be extensive due to the huge cloud of dust and debris still hanging over the city.'"

Meeker thought, Holy mackerel, it worked. "Everyone was very excited and proud," he said.

Only later he found out there was an equally large plant in the state of Washington, where research on a plutonium bomb took place. He said the bomb dropped on Nagasaki Aug. 9 was plutonium.

In October 1945, he was sent to the laboratory at Los Alamos, N.M., to act as a security guard for three to four months before his Army discharge the next February. He was given an Army patch symbolizing his atomic research, which he wore on the sleeve of his uniform.

"It was not at all unusual to have seasoned veterans from the Pacific come up to me and see that patch and shake my hand — it might be on the street, or it might be anywhere," Meeker said. "You can well imagine what the cost in both American and Japanese lives would have been if we'd had to invade. But, then I would have said, no more (atomic) testing."

Artist drew bomb blast

Axel Axhoj

Fifty years ago, Axel Axhoj took a vacation the first week of August. Along with his wife, Gladys, and two small children, he rented a cabin on Gilbert Lake.

Though he worked full time at the Scintilla plant in Sidney, Axhoj moonlighted as an illustrator for The Oneonta Star. When Eugene J. Brown, then editor and general manager, needed a drawing for a cartoon or an advertisement, he called Axhoj.

Relaxing at the lake on Aug. 6, 1945, Axhoj had no idea an atomic bomb had been dropped on Japan. But, of course, Eugene Brown got word to him.

"All these log cabins are out there, way in the woods and suddenly, out of nowhere, here was Gene Brown, coming up from Oneonta. He's been chasing all over town trying to find me," said Axhoj, who now lives in Otego.

"He was all out of breath and he said, 'We dropped an atomic bomb and I've got to have a picture, I've got to have it now. I've got to have it in the paper tomorrow morning.'"

It was dusk, and the men drove to the Star office, where they talked about what an atomic bomb might look like — but neither had the faintest idea.

Axhoj went to his house, then on Oneonta's Winney Hill Road, and drew for an hour.

"It must have been about 10 o'clock when I got done with this. ... I went back to his office and he was waiting for me. He said, 'Just fine' and he rushed out."

The drawing appeared on page 2 in the Aug. 7 edition. An editorial opinion on page 4 was titled "End of War Or Civilization."

With little more knowledge than the fact an atomic bomb had been dropped, Brown and Axhoj wrongly guessed that the target must have been Tokyo. Only later they learned it hit Hiroshima.

"All he knew was that we had dropped a bomb, period. He was so excited about it; and I don't blame him," he said. "He felt it was his job to have that news in the paper tomorrow morning. Don't forget, in those days we didn't have TVs. ... We all depended on the newspapers."

The original pen and ink drawing, about 10 by 12 inches, was later discarded. And the pay? He got $10.

Victory Over Japan

World War II ends with prayer, jubilation

Train whistles screamed and church bells rang 50 years ago today, spreading the news. Japan's Emperor Hirohito had announced unconditional surrender over Japanese radio, bringing the nightmare of the second World War to a close.

Betty Clemons was 22 then.

"It was evening, and I heard it on the radio, on WGY," said Clemons, who still lives in Oneonta. "Everybody went crazy; they were all calling each other on the telephone. There were a lot of tears, I'm sure. A few classmates of mine at St. Mary's had been killed, and I had a brother who was stationed in India."

Yet, perhaps the greatest relief was felt by the men and women who would have invaded Japan. Harris Clark Jr. of Cooperstown had been conducting bombing raids over the Japanese mainland since May of 1945 in a B-29, the biggest of America's bombers.

Stationed on Tinian in the Mariana Islands, Clark was pilot on 35 missions, the last one July 29. As part of the 21st Air Force, 468th Bomb Group, he dropped both demolition bombs and incendiary bombs, which contained napalm to start fires.

"Whatever that napalm struck, it would stick to and burn," Clark said. "And so, we just burned all the cities up in Japan."

Every three or four days he and his crew were sent out on missions, which lasted 15 or 16 hours round-trip. They bombed Osaka, Kobe and a host of other cities. On some missions, "pathfinder" planes led the way.

"They dropped a 50-gallon barrel of napalm and that would light up the area, would give us the target," he said. "Different wings, different groups would have different targets."

When they weren't in the air, life in the Pacific wasn't much fun for the 22-year-old Clark.

"I never saw an officer's club or an enlisted man's club from the time I left the States 'til I got to Hawaii (going home)," he said. "We didn't have no movies; we had one USO show in India. There was no bars, no restaurants, no dance halls; there was no girls, there was nothing. I think the most fun we had was one of the crews had a pet bear." So they played with "Gertie."

During one of his last missions against Singapore, over the Malay peninsula, Clark's plane called "Fast Company" was shot up and he had to crash land.

"The navigator was wounded and we lost an engine," he said. "Out of the four planes that went over the target — that was one formation — the lead plane was shot down." Crew from another shot-up plane bailed out over islands up the coast from Singapore, while the third plane landed on a dirt strip in Burma.

"We got back to the base and we couldn't get our left (landing) gear down. We had no flaps, no brakes, so we crash-landed," he said. "Just three weeks to the day after that, we took it up for a test flight. They put it all back together."

In late July as Clark was finishing up his missions, Bill Davis of Oneonta arrived on Tinian, as a radio operator on a B-29 in the 8th Air Force. At age 19, he'd just finished training after graduating from Sidney High School.

Harris Clark Jr. holds a copy of The Daily Star from May 1945 that features a story about bombing raids similar to the ones he piloted in a B-29. Clark is wearing his original Army uniform jacket. (Photo by Julie Lewis)

"As soon as the airfield was finished in Okinawa, we were to be assigned there, to start bombing the Japanese," Davis said. "We were so greatly relieved when they surrendered."

By September 1945, he was stationed on Okinawa and was at the airfield when a Japanese peace envoy landed on its way to the Philippines to negotiate the surrender.

On Sept. 2, the formal surrender papers were signed on the battleship USS *Missouri* in Tokyo Bay. Foreign Minister Mamoru Shigemitsu and Army Chief of Staff General Umezu signed for Japan, while General Douglas MacArthur signed as Allied Supreme Commander, Admiral Chester W. Nimitz for the United States, Admiral Sir Bruce Fraser for Britain and General Sir Thomas Blamey for Australia.

About 2,000 Allied planes roared over the Missouri in a show of strength, with Davis in his B-29.

Later, as a crew member for Gen. Patrick Timberlake, Davis flew all over the Far East, including to MacArthur's headquarters in Tokyo that fall.

"We were in Japan shortly after the surrender," he said. "It really wasn't as devastating as I thought it would be. A lot of it was flattened and burned, but still, public transportation was running and it was functioning better than I thought it would under the circumstances."

William Davis with B-29 model. (Photo by Julie Lewis)

Surrender spells relief for sailors

Japan's surrender spelled relief for David Colliton, as it did for thousands of Allied sailors. A metalsmith and welder in the Damage Control Division aboard the heavy cruiser USS *Chester*, Colliton was in the Aleutian Islands when the surrender was announced.

"It was pretty quiet," he said at his Laurens home. "We couldn't celebrate, like everybody else. But we were happy."

Colliton and his group were uneasy about the Japanese they now encountered. He had been with Task Force 8 returning to Pearl Harbor in December 1941 when Japan first attacked. Scheduled to be there Dec. 6, the ships were delayed refueling at sea by bad weather and entered Pearl Harbor Dec. 8.

"It was just a terrible mess," he said. "You could hardly get in there; we left there shortly after that."

Colliton saw disaster in other forms. Supporting Army and Marine landings on numerous Pacific islands, the Chester was bombarded by Japanese batteries and planes. Part of an armada of 21 ships raiding the Japanese in the Marshall and Gilbert Islands in early 1942, a bomb hit the Chester's well deck, killing eight men and injuring 38.

In October of that year an enemy torpedo hit the ship while it was heading toward the Solomon Islands.

"It was a real moonlit night," he said. "It was about nine o'clock at night and we'd just gotten mail aboard. I was way up on deck reading mail. We just felt a terrible shock."

Sirens sounded for "general quarters" and everyone ran to battle stations.

"It took out one engine room and two fire rooms, that give the power to the engine rooms," he said. Eleven men were killed in the blast that created a 30 by 40-foot hole in the ship, and the rooms were sealed off to keep water from the rest of the cruiser.

"You just close the hatches and batten down and sometimes shore 'em up, if there's too much pressure. You take 2-by-6s or 2-by-8s and reinforce (the doors)," he said.

David Colliton
1941

After returning to Epiritu Santo for repairs, the crew witnessed the sinking of the SS *President Coolidge* that struck a mine as it entered the harbor. The Chester's crew picked up 400 survivors, while many others swam to shore.

In addition, Colliton's ship provided support for troops on Tarawa, Saipan, Guam and Iwo Jima. The Chester also had two catapults for sending spotter planes off for reconnaissance.

Part of Cruiser Division 5, the Chester was ordered to Adak, Alaska on Aug. 8, 1945, to prepare for an invasion of Japan from the north. After the surrender was announced, the ship sailed to the harbor of Ominato, Japan, on the northern part of the island of Honshu.

"We stayed there about three or four weeks," he said. "The Japanese used to come out with their barges and pick up our garbage."

Friends Opened Door To War History

If it weren't for Ilse and Jonas Wolff, I might not have written about World War II. I met them about 30 years ago, through their daughter, Miriam, who went to school and Girl Scouts with me. I found Ilse's slight German accent intriguing as a child, and I still love to hear her speak.

But, it may not have been until my teen-age years that I realized the Wolffs fled Nazi Germany. Knowing as I did almost nothing about the war, even that didn't mean much to me until my senior year in high school when Ilse came and spoke to my class. She had decided to tell her personal story, to educate youth about what bigotry can do.

She was raised in the city of Kaiserslautern, Germany, not far from the French border, in the late 1920s and early '30s. As anti-Semitic feeling increased from the early '30s on, her life, with millions of others, became uncomfortable. Men in brown shirts stood with placards in front of her father's leather business, telling shoppers not to buy from Jews.

Friends and longtime hired help were forced by law to sever contact with her family. On Kristallnacht, or Chrystal Night, Nov. 9, 1938, Jewish homes were invaded all across Germany, with people attacked, jailed and sent to concentration camps. Mobs of strangers raced through Ilse's home, smashing furniture and looting.

After escaping with her mother and grandmother, 14-year-old Ilse was hidden with her family by a hotel manager who knew her father through business. In June of 1939, the teen-age girl left Cologne, Germany, with other children in a Kindertransport, or children's transport, arranged by a committee for emigrants, that took her through Holland to England. Little did she know that Jonas Wolff, whom she would marry, also fled to England from his hometown of Mannheim.

She never saw her grandmother again, or her Uncle Robert. Many family members perished in the camps. Jonas lost both his parents.

Hearing this story was an education, but the past seemed far away and I remember feeling sad, but not shocked. Ilse also worked in the Foreign Language Department at my school in Niskayuna, just outside Schenectady, so her face was familiar to my classmates and me. Seeing her in the hall days after hearing her story kept the ideas in our minds.

Jonas and Ilse Wolff

But, the shocking part was seeing the film.

A short time after Ilse's talk, my class was shown a documentary movie that is the only other thing I recall being taught about World War II in school. As the film began in black and white, the narrator's voice said that the film contained actual footage of Nazi concentration camps, along with descriptions of atrocities performed by German doctors. At that point, I heard my friend Miriam say, "I can't watch this; these were my relatives" and leave the room.

During the more than 20 years since, Ilse has continued to speak with youth about the Holocaust. On April 23 she received the 1995 Educational Outreach Award, along with other lecturers, from the Holocaust Survivors & Friends Education Center in Latham.

Jonas, who is a more private person, appeared with Ilse for the first time this year at one of her presentations. They have both written memoirs of their growing up years, so their children and grandchildren will know the family history.

Perhaps the most inspiring part to me is that neither one of them is bitter. They remember their beautiful times in Germany: hearing mother play Mozart on piano; eating cookies at holiday time. As German natives themselves, they know the best and the worst the country had to offer them in those days.

By sharing their stories, the Wolffs and others like them help the rest of us to grow. If we didn't live through an experience, we can't truly know what it was like. But as I've heard other tales from airplane pilots, sailors and soldiers on the line, the pieces start to fall into place.

On Memorial Day we honor the millions who have died in all of our wars. May we follow the example of those who have been there, and not be bitter, but hopeful. The only way to go now is forward.

Index

Printed in the USA
CPSIA information can be obtained
at www.ICGtesting.com
JSHW060056150824
68134JS00032B/2746